# The Strater Hotel Story

*Durango's Premier Landmark*
*"The Jewel of the Rockies"*

Philip A. Aleo

# The Strater Hotel Story
*Durango's Premier Landmark*
*"The Jewel of the Rockies"*

Copyright © 2009 By Philip A. Aleo
All Rights Reserved

ISBN 978-0-578-04237-4

Published By Aleo Publications,
Division of P.F.C. Supply Co. Inc.
P.O. Box 1085
Dundee IL 60118

Cover Photo:  Jonas Grushkin / PhotoGenesis
Jonas@Grushkin.com / www.Grushkin.com
Durango, Colorado

Printed in the United States of America

Printed by Carlith Printers

# Contents

# Personal Note from the Author

Colorado is a destination that everyone should make within their lifetime. For those of you that have visited this state; been able to travel into the majestic Rocky mountains; breathe in the crisp clean air and feel at one with the earth as I do when I come to Colorado; you know what I mean when I call it "love at first sight." Having traveled throughout the United States, Mexico and Europe, there are few places that have captured my heart as Colorado has. I have made the journey from my home in Illinois to this state almost once a year since my first visit in 1996.

In early 2006, while charting out my plans for my yearly vacation to Colorado, I decided to revisit Mesa Verde, the Indian cliff dwellings of the Anasazi (also and more properly known as the Ancestral Puebloans). The cliff dwellings date as far back as 700 A.D. If you haven't had the opportunity to visit Mesa Verde, I highly recommend that you do so. Mesa Verde has been selected as the number one historic monument in the world by readers of Conde Nast Traveler and was chosen by National Geographic Traveler as one of the *"50 places of a Lifetime - The World's Greatest Destinations."*

The decision was made to stay in Durango because of its close proximity to Mesa Verde. Browsing the web, I came across the Strater Hotel. The charm and atmosphere as viewed through the pictures on the web, definitely caught my attention. After reviewing the information on the Strater, I made immediate arrangements to stay there during my visit to nearby Mesa Verde.

In August of 2006, I made my journey into Colorado and eventually pulled into Durango. When I walked through the ornate entrance of the Strater, it was as though I had stepped back in time. My appreciation and enthusiasm must have been clearly evident, because, one of the employees at the front desk offered right there on the spot to give me a personal tour of the hotel. As we walked the halls and entered the various rooms, my heart began to race. I was absorbing the dignity, charm and character of this grand hotel that has occupied this space for over 120 years!

Upon completion of the tour, I asked the kind employee named Rick, if there was any literature regarding the Strater available for purchase. He thought for a moment, and then perked up and said, "Yes, in fact, there is a small brochure that was actually just found recently in storage." He searched in a number of locations and then came up with a red velvet covered booklet entitled, *"The Strater Hotel Story"* by Marion Jarvis, first published in 1963. I immediately went to my room and devoured the contents of this publication.

The booklet reinforced my inward feelings that the history of this hotel is as unique as its beauty, character and fine craftsmanship. The Strater has held on to the charm and warmth that it has maintained since its opening day in 1888. However, being a published author who loves history as well as photography, I knew that I wanted to have a part in producing a new book for Durango and the Strater. With digital technology on my side, coupled with the events of an additional 45 years; this grand historical monument was begging for a *new* book to be produced, that would showcase the Strater as it stands today.

Continued on next page

This new book includes details regarding the birth of Colorado as a state, as well as the birth and development of Durango in 1881. I then go on to explain how this paved the way for Henry Strater to build the Strater Hotel in 1887.

It is my hope that this book plants a seed within your heart, that will grow into the love affair that I have with my favorite destination, Durango, Colorado and the Strater Hotel.

Philip A. Aleo

**This is a photo of the original red velvet cover of the 61 page booklet entitled *The Strater Hotel Story* that Marion Jarvis wrote in 1963. Marion's research and documentation formed the foundation for the information surrounding the early history of the Strater Hotel.**

# Acknowledgements

*First and foremost,* I thank Mr. Roderick E. Barker; the Owner, President and CEO of the Strater Hotel for his enthusiasm and open handed assistance provided to me. If not for Rod, this book would not have been possible.

*I also thank:.........*

The staff at the Strater Hotel that was always available, kind and professional during my extended stays at the Strater doing research and writing.

Mr. Barker's grandmother, Marion Jarvis. The 61 page booklet she wrote and published in 1963 formed the foundation for this new and expanded version.

The Animas Museum for their historical information and photos that have complimented the written and photographic history of early Durango.

Betty Strater Albrecht and her cousin Carol Strater for their assistance with the history of their family and also sharing family photographs that were taken in Durango more than 125 years ago. These have been an immense aid to the reconstruction of time and events in the early history of Durango.

Greg Stilwell for sharing many memories of his grandfather, Charles, who ran the Strater a century ago, as well as providing photographs that have aided so much in compiling the Strater Hotel Story.

So many members of the Durango area have given of their time in interviews. I thank all of you so very much! Individuals including Arvo Matis who is 101 years old at the time of our interview; Fred Kroeger who was raised in Durango and was 92 years old at the time of our interview; Charlie Schumacher, Dennis Johnson and others.

I especially wanted to express my appreciation to Duane Smith, perhaps the most knowledge-able historian of Durango history alive today. We spent an entire evening together in an interview that was very enlightening. Mr. Smith has written and published 48 books on Colorado History. These masterpieces have woven a comprehensive history of this area that is truly amazing. He kindly gave me permission to use anything that he had written to further my purpose with this unique history of the Strater Hotel. Duane, thank you so much!

The Cleveland Public Library and their vast reservoir of historical records that added so much detail to the early history of the Strater family.

The Durango Public Library was instrumental in that they have the local newspapers on microfilm going back to the infancy of Durango. These proved very helpful in locating advertisements and other data regarding the Strater Hotel, the Strater Drug store, as well as information on the Strater family.

The Website www.coloradohistoricnewspapers.org was a great resource for locating various newspaper articles dated between 1871 and 1923. I thank the staff and researchers who have put this site together and made it available to the public.

June Hahl was so gracious in offering her assistance. With her professional journalistic background, she gave of her time and experience proofreading the book. Thank you so much June!

If I have forgotten to make mention of any other persons that have assisted me, I sincerely apologize. It was not intentional. So many people have stepped forward and provided assistance and encouragement. Thank you all so very much!.

# Chapter One
1

# A Snapshot of Colorado in the 1800's

# A Snapshot of Colorado in the 1800's

*On the middle 1800's,* the population of the United States was approximately twenty three million people. The country was still in its infancy, growing and expanding at a remarkable rate. The Midwest was a focal point for most of the expansion at this time. Chicago, Illinois was a highlight and a focal point for many. Chicago was incorporated as a town on August 4th, 1833. The population at the time was merely 550 people. By 1850, Chicago had grown to 30,000 people! By 1854, the population reached 80,000.

St. Louis, "The Gateway to the West", increased 372% in just 10 years from 1840 to 1850 to a population of 77,860.

On January 4th 1848, John Sutter discovered gold in California. He attempted to keep the discovery of gold secret to avoid prospectors, but word got out. On December 5, 1848, President James Polk, speaking to Congress, confirmed accounts of the discovery of gold in California. This became national news. Immediately thereafter in 1849, the California Gold Rush began. In 1850 alone, some 2,800 steamboats arrived at St. Louis filled with pioneers seeking a new life out west. St. Louis had become the second largest port in the country. [1]

William Greeneberry Russell, from Georgia, had worked in the California gold fields in the 1850's. Russell was married to an Indian woman from the Cherokee tribe. It was through his connections to the Cherokee tribe that he heard about a discovery of gold back in 1849 along the South Platte River of Colorado.[2] The South Platte River drains much of the eastern flank of the Rocky Mountains in Colorado.

In February of 1858, Russell organized a group and set out westward in pursuit of wealth and riches. On May 23rd of 1858, Russell and his party reached Cherry Creek and the South Platte. The site of their initial exploration is in present day Confluence Park, located in Denver, Colorado. They were unsuccessful for more than 5 weeks. Then in the first week of July, Mr. Russell, along with Sam Bates, found a small placer deposit of gold near the mouth of Little Dry Creek.[3] The site is located today in present day Englewood, a suburb of Denver. Their first discovery of gold weighed in at 20 troy ounces or 622 grams. In the 1850's, the value of one troy ounce of gold was $20.67. The average worker made around six dollars and fifty cents per week ($6.50). This initial discovery valued at around four hundred ten dollars in 1858, would have taken the average worker almost fifteen months to earn! At the time of this writing, gold is priced out at $1,031 per troy ounce. Their initial discovery would be valued at just over $20,620 in today's dollars. This is the first significant discovery of gold in the Rocky Mountain Region.

The Pike's Peak Gold Rush (later known as the Colorado Gold Rush) began. The Colorado Gold Rush encompassed the Pike's Peak Country of the northwestern Kansas Territory [(1)] and also part of the Nebraska Territory [(2)] of the United States that was established in July 1858 and lasted roughly until the creation of the Colorado Territory on February 28, 1861. These "territories" were what preceded the eventual States that were to follow.

An estimated 100,000 gold seekers took part in the Colorado Gold Rush, the greatest gold rush in North American history. When you consider the total population of the United States at the time which was twenty three million, 100,000 people is a considerable number. The participants in the gold rush were known as the "Fifty-Niners" after 1859, the peak year of the rush.[4]

# A Snapshot of Colorado in the 1800's

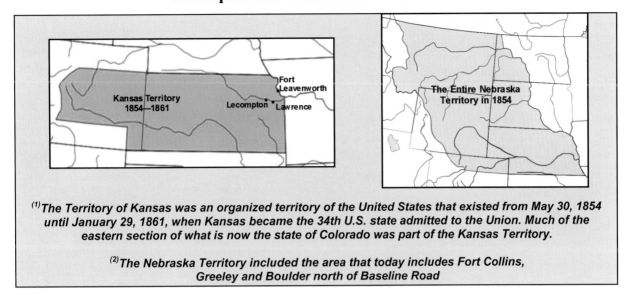

<sup>(1)</sup>*The Territory of Kansas was an organized territory of the United States that existed from May 30, 1854 until January 29, 1861, when Kansas became the 34th U.S. state admitted to the Union. Much of the eastern section of what is now the state of Colorado was part of the Kansas Territory.*

<sup>(2)</sup>*The Nebraska Territory included the area that today includes Fort Collins, Greeley and Boulder north of Baseline Road*

Up until that time, the Durango area had seen few Anglo–Europeans. The few that did come through this area were trappers, traders or explorers. Up until the mid 1800's, this area had been occupied by the Ute Indians, also known as Noochew. Ute means "Land of the Sun". [5]

In the spring of 1860, Charles Baker and a prospecting party of fifteen men were exploring the mountains around the area where today the town of Silverton flourishes. They knew that they were in hostile Ute Indian territory, to increase their chances for survival, they split up into three separate groups. One of the groups was located by the Ute's and killed. This didn't deter the others. They came upon gold and in no time set up camp and named the settlement Baker's Park. It held this name for thirteen years. Today we know it as Silverton.

Mining into the mountains was difficult. The veins ran deep, making the gold difficult to reach. It required extensive tunneling and ore processing. Once it was mined, transportation was extremely slow and difficult. The dangers of mining are evident by the hundreds of graves still located around the mining towns of the 1800's. Something was sorely lacking that would greatly benefit the miners and others attempting to live in the mountainous regions of Colorado. What was needed was the "Iron Horse." Thankfully, "The General", William Jackson Palmer was on the horizon!

## General William Jackson Palmer
## Entrepreneur Extraordinaire

*William Jackson Palmer*

If there was one man who stood out regarding the growth and development of the West, especially Colorado, it was William Jackson Palmer. He was born in the state of Delaware in Kent County on September 17th, 1836. When he was five years old, his family moved to Philadelphia. In 1853, at the early age of seventeen, Palmer went to work for the Engineering Corps of the Hempfield Railroad. At the age of nineteen, he traveled to Europe, including France and England to study railroading and also coal mining. He went to Europe with endorsements by a number of influential personages, one of whom was the President of the Pennsylvania Railroad, J. Edgar Thompson. Palmer stayed in

# A Snapshot of Colorado in the 1800's

Europe to study for about one year. Upon his return in July of 1856, he worked directly under J. Edgar Thompson as his personal secretary.

His career in the railroad business was interrupted in 1861 with the Civil War. Being raised as a Quaker, Palmer had a strong disregard for violence and war, but this was tempered with a strong passion for justice. He truly was indignant regarding the issue of slavery, and was passionate regarding their rights and freedom. Because of this, he joined the Union Army and made a reputable name for himself. Palmer led many successful campaigns and proved himself from the onset to be a strong leader. At the young age of 29 in 1865, he became the second youngest Brigadier General commissioned in the Civil War, second only to General Custer.

The end of the war in 1865 allowed Palmer to return to his first love—the railroad. He initially worked for the Union Pacific Railroad, Eastern Division. In 1867, he was part of a survey party whose responsibility was to find the best route for construction of a railroad that would run from Kansas City to California. Although the Union Pacific never accomplished this feat, the idea was firmly implanted in Palmer's mind.

In 1869, the Eastern Division of the Union Pacific Railroad became the Kansas Pacific Railroad. William Jackson Palmer was elected as one of its directors in charge of railroad construction with the purpose of extending the line to Denver Colorado. As Palmer scouted the eastern face of the Rockies, he came to the Pikes Peak area near present day Colorado Springs. The beauty of this area left him in awe. He had never before seen such beautiful views as those from Pikes Peak, or the unique majesty and grandeur of what is known today as The Garden of the Gods located in Colorado Springs.

*The Garden of the Gods, Colorado Springs, Colo. Sandstone rock formations rising over 500 feet can be viewed throughout the State Park. This was originally part of William Jackson Palmer's property in the 1870's.*

# A Snapshot of Colorado in the 1800's

It was here that Palmer would build his estate and begin his family with the woman who had won his heart, the beautiful Mary Lincoln Mellen. Palmer's wife was the daughter of one of his business associates, William Proctor Mellen. For a time, Mr. Mellen worked within the government for the Secretary of the Treasury. Later, he opened up a private practice as a lawyer in New York City. It was in St Louis on a business trip, that he introduced his daughter nicknamed "Queen" to William Palmer. They were married in 1870.

After their four month honeymoon to Europe, it was Palmer's intention to settle in what would later become Colorado Springs. He purchased 10,000 acres of land for $12,500 ($1.25 per acre). This may seem like a small sum by today's standards, however, when you consider that the average wage in the United States in 1870 was just $350 per year, the price of $12,500 changes perspective. It would have taken a common citizen in this country 35 years to even make that much money! Adding to the reality that the average life expectancy of a male Caucasian in 1870 was around 40 years of age, these combined factors help us to appreciate the caliber of success Palmer had attained by the age of 34.

Palmer also purchased an additional 2,225 acres of land near the Garden of the Gods. It was here that he built his original 22 room dream home. He eventually named his estate Glen Eyrie. The estate and home flourish to this day. The Glen Eyrie Group, the camp and conference ministry of the Navigators, own and operate the estate today.

*William Jackson Palmer's home which he named "Glen Eyrie" (Meaning Valley of the Eagle's Nest in Scottish) was completed in February of 1872. He had the original wooden structure encased with carefully selected stones from Bear Canyon in 1903. The stone walls were built without chisel or mallet on the surfaces of the stone, because the General did not want the moss or the lichen disturbed. The castle had 65 rooms, a drawing room for the ladies, a library, a den, and a large dining hall. There were Turkish baths, a milk room for the dairy maids, and a special ice-cream room filled with ice making machinery. On the top of the tower was a roof garden where a large bell was hung. This bell had come from Germany, weighing one ton, and when rung, could be heard for six miles. Palmer also built many other unique items into the castle, including secret panels, tunnels, fire extinguishers hidden in the walls and indirect lighting.* [6]

# A Snapshot of Colorado in the 1800's

In 1871 Palmer founded Colorado Springs (originally named Fountain Colony). Palmer loved this land and cared about the residents that lived here. He did many humanitarian acts that benefit us even to this day. Here are a few examples:

1. He reserved land and contributed funds for the purpose of a college. Present day Colorado College sits on this site.
2. Lots were given to any persons or group who wanted to build a church.
3. To avoid the beauty of the area from being harmed, he didn't allow the removal of any trees in the area named today, the Garden of the Gods. Instead, he brought in 600 trees from the banks of the Arkansas River to plant along the wide streets.[7]
4. In 1902 Palmer donated 100 acres and $50,000 for a Sanatorium, a place for treatment, rehabilitation and therapy of the chronically ill.
5. In 1907, "the General" donated 480 acres in the upper Cañon, including Helen Hunt and Silver Cascade Falls, along with the "High Drive" that leads to Bear Creek Regional Park.

*The first "Baby Train" as it was called because of the narrow gauge.*

*State Historical Society of Colorado*

## The Denver and Rio Grande Railroad

1870 was marked by major events in General Palmer's life. Not only did he marry, he also founded the Denver and Rio Grande Railroad (D&RG). It was his intention that this railroad extend from Denver all the way down to Mexico.

As he continued to extend his railroad southward along the eastern face of the majestic Rocky Mountains, he had intentions of building branches in two directions. The first branch would intersect with the railroad that he had started in Mexico, whereas the second branch would extend up into the mountains. With his friend Dr. Bell and others, the D&RG reached Pueblo, forty-five miles south of Colorado Springs in 1872. It was here that Palmer started the Colorado Coal and Iron Company for the purpose of furnishing fuel and rails for the railroad.

The General's crews continued on, building southward. When they reached Raton Pass, approximately ninety miles south of Pueblo, trouble arose. The competing Santa Fe Railroad had brought men and teams into the mountains and also posted armed guards on the hills, to stop the D&RG workers from making any further progress. Palmer respected their position, as the law stated that: "the first to begin had the right to build". General Palmer withdrew his men and focused his interests on the other branch that he was building, which had already reached Canon City deep in the mountains, some 40 miles northwest of Pueblo and twenty miles south of Cripple Creek. Nearby, a deep gorge (now known as The Royal Gorge) had been cut into the mountains eons ago by the Arkansas River. He recognized that the spectacular beauty of this area would provide a breathtaking scenic route into the mountain country.

# A Snapshot of Colorado in the 1800's

Palmer was fully aware of the intense competition with other railroads for right of way to construct. He sent a telegram in haste to his work crews located near Trinidad at El Moro, some seventy miles south of Pueblo. He instructed them to set out immediately for the Royal Gorge to take possession. Somehow, spies for the Santa Fe Railroad intercepted the message and sent word to their engineer in charge. Setting out for Canon City on horseback from Pueblo, the engineer rode his hired horse so hard that, as he neared the city, the horse fell to the ground unable to move. Picking himself up, he left the horse and literally ran into the streets of Canon City offering high pay to every man he could find, to bring picks and shovels into the Royal Gorge.[8]

On April 19, 1878, Palmer's men arrived at the Royal Gorge. They found the Santa Fe Engineer and his crew digging, attempting to give the impression that they already were building a railroad. Now keep in mind that Palmer had been working on this branch for some time; his end of laid track was only 3/4 of a mile from Canon City. Palmer was not going to back off this time. He stated: "People have invested their money in our railroad and we must not disappoint them. I have authority from Congress to build through this Gorge. This time, we are not going to leave." This decision by Palmer had implications that have dramatically affected the development of Colorado to this day. If he would have folded under the pressure, chances are Durango, as well as other towns that he had a huge impact on, would not exist today.

Despite Palmer's stand, the Santa Fe men also refused to back down. What would Palmer do? He was a man of principle, but this was tempered with justice. He is on record as telling his family, "I do not approve of killing and useless bloodshed, but I cannot desert a just cause." [9]

He ordered his men to dig trenches, build small forts and arm themselves with guns. The rival Santa Fe officials hired six hundred men from cattle ranches and tough western towns and instructed them to shed blood if necessary. They also built forts on the opposite side of the gorge. Each side waited for the other to take the first shot. In the mean time, it was Palmer's objective to have this settled in the courts. The feud went on for two years. Men continued to man the forts on both sides. Although there were fist fights along the railroad and engineers and other workers were being pulled off the trains and beaten up, no shots were ever fired. Finally, on March 27, 1880, a telegram came across the wires at midnight stating that the D&RG could have the Royal Gorge. Celebrations ensued throughout Colorado Springs!

Palmer had his sites set on Silverton. The mineral riches of Silverton, deep in the San Juan Mountains, had been his goal since 1876. The path Palmer used to lay rails to Silverton included a tract of land 1.5 miles away from the southern boundary of a small town named Animas City, which was Junction Street. In 1879, he had two men establish what would be named "The Durango Trust." These two influential men, the Ex-Territorial Governor Alexander Hunt and a British physician named William Bell, purchased 160 acres of land for $105,000. This land was destined to become the town named Durango.

Some believe that negotiations had broken down between Animas City and Palmer's men and that is why Durango was established. Careful analysis and reconstruction of events leads others to believe that Palmer and the D&RG had the plans of a new town in mind from the start. John L. McNeil, an early pioneer who lived in the area in 1880 is on record as stating: *The D&RG*

# A Snapshot of Colorado in the 1800's

*built its own towns as it went along; Colorado Springs instead of developing Colorado City across the river; also Pueblo instead of Plaza; and Cuchara Junction, Walsenburg, Alamosa, Chama, Durango.*"[10] There were probable negotiations between Animas City and Palmer's men for the construction of a depot in Animas City. Evidently, the proposed charge of $50,000 to Animas City by Palmer was too high for them to accept and they refused. So Palmer continued on with his goal of starting Durango. They simply laid their rails right through Animas City and didn't develop a stop there. They were an enterprising group of men that knew that the money came, not from the passengers of a train, but from the towns they would start up and develop and the tracts of land that they would sell. They were real estate geniuses! The proposed town laid out by the Trust comprised of 1,780 original lots that sold for an average price of $160 dollars each. At this price, the $105,000 dollar investment would grow to $284,800 dollars or 270%. This is comparable to a profit of nearly eighteen million dollars in today's terms! (Based upon the fact that the value of one dollar back in 1880 was one hundred times greater than today.)

What was their motive? Enterprise! They intended to use this location and the town they would build as the railhead[*] for the Denver and Rio Grande Railroad. Who were these two men and how were they affiliated with the railroad?

Alexander Hunt was born in New York City on January 12, 1825. At the age of 25 he left for California seeking wealth and fortune. Initially, he did quite well financially even though the 1850's was a time of reduced economic activity. The country was in a recession. Matters in the nation continued to worsen in 1857, leading to "The Financial Panic of 1857," which threw the entire nation into a depression that didn't end till the outbreak of the Civil War.

When the depression hit, it decimated Alexander Hunt financially. He decided to move his family out of California and headed eastward to what would become the Colorado Territory. The Colorado Territory had its share of outlaws raising havoc on the small settlements and the pioneer families moving west. Shortly after his arrival, Hunt was chosen to be the judge of a vigilante removal committee. The purpose of this committee was to remove the outlaws from the Territory. Their favorite tool for bringing the vigilantes to justice was hangings. Within a few years, Hunt became a US Marshall of the newly formed "Colorado Territory." After serving as US Marshall for about five years, he became the Territorial Governor of the Colorado Territory on April 24, 1867. It was a personal appointment by President Andrew Jackson, and he remained Governor for about two years. In 1870, he became one of the key players in the development of the Rio Grande Railway Company, founded by Palmer. Hunt was appointed President of the "Rio Grande Extension," the construction division of the company. He was instrumental with the inception of Durango, and in fact, is credited with giving the town its name.

The other person affiliated with the 'Durango Trust' was Dr. William Bell, a wealthy physician from England, who had become a very close friend to Palmer. He not only personally invested in the railroad, he assisted in raising capital for the D&RG. He also loved the American West. It was Dr. Bell that chose the location for the town of Durango and also oversaw the platting

---

[*]A railhead is the final destination of a railway line that interfaces with another mode of transport. So Durango was to become a prominent city because of it's being designated as the railhead.

# A Snapshot of Colorado in the 1800's

and design of the new town.

Hunt and Bell's plans, along with those of Palmer, came to fruition on July 27th 1881 when the D&RG Railroad completed construction of its tracks to Durango. On August 5th, 1881 the first train rolled into town with General Palmer, the Governor of Colorado and three former Governors on board.

*I took this photo on-board the Durango & Silverton Railroad*
*heading up to Silverton from Durango in 2006.*

Within weeks of this date, construction of tracks to Silverton began. By July of 1882, just 11 months later, the tracks to Silverton were completed. Taking into consideration the distance between Durango and Silverton, the terrain that had to be overcome and the tools used to accomplish this feat, this accomplishment truly testifies to man's ability to overcome insurmountable obstacles!

These hard working men laid a total of 45 miles of track through the mountains using primitive tools including hand saws, black powder, picks and shovels. Consider the ramifications of what this entailed! Every day, on the average for 330 days straight, they not only cleared away brush and cut down trees, they also "blasted" their way through the solid rock mountains using black powder. They then prepared, graded and laid a daily average of 720 feet of track! The wages received was considered a generous wage for the time, - $2.25 per day. In the 1880's, the average worker in the U.S. was making just $6.50 per week, or a little more than one dollar a day based upon the average 6 day work week.

# A Snapshot of Colorado in the 1800's

The street side view (Main Avenue) of the Durango Railway Station. Photo circa 1890. Note the trolley tracks in the foreground.

*Courtesy of the La Plata County Historical Society*

The original Durango Train Station was built in 1881 and has been used without interruption ever since. This color photo was taken in April, 2009.

# A Snapshot of Colorado in the 1800's

*The Durango & Silverton just south of Hermosa Creek and north of Durango.*
*Courtesy of Michael R. Ripley*

# A Snapshot of Colorado in the 1800's

The narrow gauge railroad tracks from Durango to Silverton follow the Animas River through the mountains.

*Engine 481 at milepost 484.4, one of the last of two remaining wooden water tanks on the Durango and Silverton. The Needleton Tank hasn't been in service since the 1960's.* Courtesy of Michael R. Ripley

# A Snapshot of Colorado in the 1800's

**Winter scene of the High Line curve**    *Courtesy of Michael R. Ripley*

**Locomotives 480 and 481 powering up at the Durango Train Depot.**
*Courtesy of Roderick E Barker*

# A Snapshot of Colorado in the 1800's

*There are two factors that have had a huge impact on Durango in the past, as well as the present. The Railroad and the Strater Hotel. This scene, capturing a locomotive at the switch track with the Strater in the background has not changed in the past 122 years. In fact, engine 480 has been in Durango and on these tracks since 1925. It was built for the D&RG by the Baldwin Locomotive Works in Philadelphia. It was one of ten built. These were the last narrow gauge locomotives ever built in the United States.*

*Courtesy of Michael R. Ripley*

# A Snapshot of Colorado in the 1800's

*This photo of the Durango Railway Station and Engine 470 was taken in the 1930's.*
*Courtesy La Plata County Historical Society*

Although the railroad played a major role in the development of Colorado, people needed the ability to travel on land with their horse or mule drawn wagons as well. This presented problems in the Colorado territory, particularly when it came to overcoming a major obstacle—the Rocky Mountains. There happens to be a very special man that possessed the desire, ability, insight and finances to overcome this obstacle. This man was Otto Mears.

## Otto Mears (1840—1931)

Southern Colorado owes much to this unique man. He was born in Kurland, Russia on May 3, 1840 and orphaned by the age of three years old. He lived with an uncle for about six years. Already having 12 children of his own, the Uncle arranged for Otto to live with another relative residing in New York. It took weeks on the ocean to get from Europe to New York. Within a number of months, Otto was being sent to live with yet another relative located in California. To get from New York to California, he was put onto a steamer heading south in the Atlantic toward Panama. The Panama Canal didn't exist at the time, so, upon his arrival, he rode on horseback for about fifty or sixty miles to the Pacific Coast. Otto then boarded another boat that eventually arrived in San Francisco. Upon his arrival, he faced two major problems; he only spoke Russian and the relative that he had come to live with was not there. He had left the country for Australia![11]

So Otto was left to fend for himself at the age of ten. He wasn't afraid

*Otto Mears*

# A Snapshot of Colorado in the 1800's

to tackle anything. He did everything from selling newspapers and milking cows to learning to work with metals as a tinsmith. This tough childhood tempered him into a man of insight and fortitude.

At 19 years of age he was working in the gold fields of California and Nevada. During the Civil War, he fought in the Navajo Wars under the command of Kit Carson. While in the army, the Quartermaster asked him if he knew how to bake bread. His answer: "Yes," although he truly had no experience whatsoever. So, confidently, he assumed the extra duty of making bread, and the Quartermaster, not knowing better, gave him a pound of flour for every pound of bread he made! He sold the extra flour to the Indians, and by the time he was discharged, he'd pocketed $1,500. [12]

Combining the "bread" money with his discharge money of $400, he opened a store in Saguache located about 170 miles northeast of Durango in the San Luis Valley. In order to enlarge the store, he needed lumber, so he constructed the first lumber mill in SW Colorado. To satisfy the demand for flour, he planted 200 acres of wheat. Not satisfied with harvesting by hand and threshing with sheep, he brought in the first mower, reaper and threshing machine to the area, and built the first grist mill as well. By harvest, the Government's purchase price had dropped from $20 per hundred pounds to $5. He decided to freight his crop to the gold camp of California Gulch (Leadville, Colorado) 100 miles north. There were no roads over Poncha Pass and his wagons floundered in the mud and rough terrain, spilling the wheat. A lone rider on horseback happened along named, William Gilpin, who had been the first Governor of the Colorado Territory in 1861-1862. Gilpin suggested that Mears build a toll road across the pass, *"You can make a lot of money"* he said. Taking the suggestion to heart and after he sold the flour for $12 per hundred pounds, Mears continued onto Denver and obtained the right to build a toll road. One had only to specify the terminal points of the road, pay five dollars for the charter and a franchise was awarded for twenty years. This started Otto Mears on his way, earning him the title he has held on to till this day, -"The Pathfinder of the San Juan."[13]

Mears' first road consisted of 50 miles over his "wheat wagon route" from Saguache to Nathrop where it connected with the road that ran from California Gulch to Denver. From collecting tolls and freighting cargo for others, he recouped his road construction expense in a few months. He then built a second road from Saguache to Lake City, northeast of Silverton. Mears later extended this road on to Silverton. In 1875, Mears was granted the contract to deliver mail to Ouray. In the winter the mail was transported by dogs pulling toboggans and the mailman on ski's. "Mail" consisted of anything and everything: tobacco, coffee, sugar, dry goods and ladies' hats; the mailman was under strict orders not to ride atop the toboggans.[14]

To facilitate transportation from Silverton to Ouray, Mears worked eight years to complete what is now named the "Million Dollar Highway". The first eight and a half miles from Ouray cost $40,000 a mile to build. The roadbed on this section was blasted out of solid rock on a thousand foot-high shelf. The name "Million Dollar Highway" came about when the State took over the road in the 1920's and spent over a million dollars per mile rebuilding six miles of the road. Others say that the name came from the belief that there is over a million dollars in gold ore mixed in with the fill dirt.

# A Snapshot of Colorado in the 1800's

*This photo of what is today named the "Million Dollar Highway" was taken in the 1880's. Viewing the "road" ahead, it is no wonder that these men had paused. I would personally really question the importance of my purpose in contemplating this path, wouldn't you? This photo was in the personal collection of the Strater Family and is believed to be two of their relatives, possibly Henry Strater to the right in the light jacket, along with his brother Frank, to the left.*     *Courtesy of Carol Strater*

The 450 miles of toll roads constructed by Otto Mears cost $325,000. His freighting business (the original UPS) earned this sum many times over. When the deep snow in the winter made supplies scarce, a ton of hay or a sack of flour could easily cost $100 each.

Otto Mears was active in the packing and freighting business from 1875 until 1890 when the railroads began to monopolize with their cheaper freight charges. By pack trains, transporting freight from Silverton to Del Norte, and on to Pueblo by wagon, cost $80 a ton. By train, it cost eight dollars a ton. The reduced cost created a bonanza for the miners and the entire region. With the establishment of the rail, the quantity of ore hauled increased from a few tons to hundreds of tons, and traffic in the form of livestock, farm produce, coal and lumber grew accordingly. Many of the railroad tracks were laid over the toll roads of Otto Mears. The Denver and Rio Grande paid Mears $40,000 for "right of way" over Marshall Pass.

From 1887 through 1891 Otto Mears built three railroads: The Silverton Railroad, the Silverton Northern Railroad, and the Rio Grande Southern; the latter of which was a spellbinding engineering accomplishment, running 172 miles from Durango to Ridgway.

There wasn't anything that Otto Mears was afraid to do. He always had the determination and the answer: *"I can do it"*- and he did! What an inspiration of a man he must have been to those with whom he shared company. He was a man with a colorful personality and a great person to have as a friend. One experience that relates his personality is at a time when he was running a

# A Snapshot of Colorado in the 1800's

*Originally built by Otto Mears in 1883, and then rebuilt by the state in 1923, this stretch of road called the "Million Dollar Highway," extends for twenty five miles and follows the route of US 550 between Silverton and Ouray. The origin of the name is disputed. Some say that it cost the state one million dollars per mile to rebuild. Others believe that the origin comes from the fact that there are millions of dollars of gold ore in the fill dirt. In this photo taken in 1948, the road is much smoother than the photo on the previous page, but the road is still extremely narrow. Note how close the wagon is to the mountain's wall! Rod Barker commented that "the hay in the back is like an extra gas tank - fuel for the horse!"*

*Courtesy of Mark L Evans*

*Northbound out of Silverton on the "Million Dollar Highway" (Route 550) toward Ouray. (April 2009)*

trading post at Saguache. A mountain man from the Wet Mountain Valley got tough and said, *"If it wasn't for your gray hairs I'd whip you!"* To which Mears replied; *"Don't let that stop you, I'll put my hat on."* The reply produced such a roar of laughter from the crowd that the mountain man just turned and walked away.[15]

Otto Mears built the first sawmill in Southwestern Colorado, he also built the first grist mill; planted the first crop of wheat in Saguache County; owned the first threshing machine; built the first road; was the first treasurer of Saguache County; carried the first mail into Ouray; dug the first irrigation ditch; built the first telegraph line in Colorado, as well as the aforementioned details regarding the toll roads and railroads.[16] We can't begin to even imagine what southwest Colorado would be like today, if it were not for the imagination, vision and drive of this one man that came to the States as an orphaned little boy from Russia in 1849. It goes without saying, that the entire mining industry and the development of Southwest Colorado owes a great debt to this one man.

Otto Mears lived out a good and long life. He passed on at the age of 91 on June 24, 1931 in Pasadena, California.

This chapter encompasses a majestic awesome country undergoing change as Anglo-Europeans filtered in from the East seeking wealth and a new life. The landscape was becoming dotted with small settlements of people. The "Iron Horse" was laying down hundreds of miles of track throughout the landscape. To their dismay, the native American Indians that had lived on this land for countless generations were being forced off.

Major changes were taking place......

*Courtesy of the La Plata County Historical Society*

# Rio Grande Southern
## RAILROAD.

The New All Rail Line To

Telluride, Placerville, Ft. Lewis, Mancos and Rico,

**NOW COMPLETED and OPEN for BUSINESS**
**From RIDGEWAY**
On the line of the Denver & Rio Grande R. R.
**To TELLURIDE**

And will be pushed to final completion to Durango and Rico by midsummer, opening up the most magnificent Scenery in the Rocky Mountains, heretofore Inaccessable and passing through the

## Famous Montezuma and Shenandoah Valleys
The Great Agricultural Region of the
**DOLORES RIVER.**

———

This new line will bring the Tourist within easy ride of the Wonderful

## Homes of the Cliff Dwellers

———

Immediate connections are made at Ridgeway with trains of the Denver & Rio Grande Railroad to and from Denver, Pueblo and Colorado Springs for Placerville and Telluride.

## Stage Connections from Telluride to Rico.

As fast as road is completed, train service will be extended, with stage connections from terminus to Rico.

**OTTO MEARS,**
General Manager.

*Otto Mears regularly ran adds in the various newspapers promoting his railroad.*

# Chapter Two
## 2

# Durango is Born

# Durango Is Born

*In 1880* the D&RG Railroad was building on to Durango. The land had already been purchased by Ex-Territorial Governor Alexander Hunt, the locating director for the railroad. According to John L. McNeil, the railroad had selected this site because of the ideal location for a smelter at the foot of Smelter Mountain. He also stated that it was the railroad's intention to establish a bank in Durango. The person that General William Jackson Palmer's agent Mr. Hunt had chosen to be the future town's agent was Jim Luttrell. John L. McNeil was one of the first persons to step into the fledgling town of Durango in 1880. He states: *"When I came, I found Jim Luttrell sitting on a pile of bricks that he had made. There was absolutely nothing in site but sage brush and sun flowers—the place was wild."(John McNeil 1849-1929)*[17]

The beauty of the San Juan Valley in the 1880's has been well documented by many pioneers for us to contemplate and reflect upon. Thanks to the *San Juan Pioneers' Association* that was originally founded in Silverton on July 6th, 1895, we have this documentation. People were eligible for membership into this association if they had arrived into the San Juan Valley prior to 1881. Its original 125 members had all lived in Conejos County (which now comprises numerous Colorado counties).

The San Juan Pioneers' Association proceeded to interview and record hundreds of accounts in the first person, and developed these accounts into four separate volumes entitled: *"Pioneers of the San Juan Country."* I have attempted to carefully analyze and record these individual experiences, and then categorize them in such a way so as to be able to provide a strikingly vivid mental photograph of the Durango area at its birth and in some instances before its birth.

The details of our ancestors have left an indelible imprint upon my heart. I am so very thankful to have the privilege of attempting to reconstruct Durango through the eyes of these original pioneers for you, the reader.

Here we go.....

When the pioneers came to this virgin territory, they found streams and springs filled with clear, cold and pure water. The scenery was and still is today difficult to give justice to. The steepest most breathtaking mountains filled with dense vegetation and colors that staggered the imagination, contrasted by the deepest gorges...with this scenery in mind, note the following:

One of the earliest settlers to come to the Durango and Animas City area was Tim McCluer. He moved his family into this area in 1875 before either town (Durango or Animas City) was ever even started. *"Upon their arrival, they found only one cabin, the ranch home of Robert Dwyer that he had built some years before. Tim had heard rumors of a cattleman's paradise over in the San Juan Basin, where there was said to be thousands of acres of rich range land surrounded by low ground covered with belly deep "wild timothy grass" with an ample supply of water close at hand.*

*He moved his family in a four horse prairie schooner loaded with supplies and food to last for months. Progress was very slow. Most of the way, roads had to be blazed, temporary bridges constructed and at some points the wagon lowered over the cliffs by ropes. The few stretches of road discernable were narrow and steep, mere shelves around the sides of mountains where it seemed that there were less than six inches of space between the vehicles occupants and eternity. Months passed before they reached the present site of Durango"*.[18]

# Durango Is Born

Louisa Rebecca Becker Jackson remembers the terribly hard trip involved in getting to Durango. Upon arrival in Durango, she expressed the beauty of the country as:

*"....another beautiful place with wildflowers, trees and berries along the river banks. Smelter Hill was a site to see, covered with trees, and gorgeous in the fall with autumn colors." (Louisa Rebecca Becker Jackson Born in 1863)*[19]

John W. Turner's parents settled in the Animas Valley before Durango was even a thought. The year was 1876. His description and recollections as a child are worth repeating. He stated:

*"I remember the Animas River when it was pure, clear water, unadulterated by mill tailings or other contaminates, flowing directly from the mountain snows, meandered through the grassy meadow lands - riffles here and deep holes there. Clean sand bars, wonderful fishing, swimming holes and boating in the summer, skating in the winter - a veritable paradise for any kid."*

*"Native pine and oak on the uplands, cottonwood and box elder along the river, and wild fruit galore everywhere. Currants, several varieties, red or squaw berries, choke berries, service berries, wild strawberries and thimble berries."*

*"There was a seemingly inexhaustible abundance of wild game, and open season the year round. Deer, ducks, grouse, rabbits and bear, as well as beaver, mink, bob cats and lynx, which provided some fine robes for winter."*[20]

John Turner stated that his father had been a part of the famous Baker Party in the exploration of Colorado back in the early 1860's prior to the Civil War breaking out. When his father heard some years later that this territory had been thrown open for settlement, he acted immediately, remembering the sheer beauty of this area.

For the people living in Animas City at the time of Durango's birth, Durango was not a welcome site. Animas City had been laid out in the summer of 1876. It was a thriving small bustling town prior to 1880, located just 1.5 miles north of where Durango would be built. One of the early pioneers in the San Juan Valley was Charles Newman. He was born in 1851 and lived in Animas City prior to Durango's establishment. He stated that *"Animas City seemed to have everything, the fertile valley, splendid location for a city, the river, mineral wealth in the hills, a moderate climate.... Even a diamond mine had been discovered! The future of this city seemed assured. But fate in the shape of a town company and the D&RG Railroad decreed otherwise. The first month of 1881 saw most business firms of Animas City moved to the new town of Durango, our own among them."*[21]

The first paper in Animas City was named the "Southwest". The Saturday May 1, 1880 issue stated regarding the coming of Durango: *"The Bank of San Juan has issued a circular in which it has stated that a branch office will be opened in the "new town of Durango on the Rio Animas". What the "new town of Durango" is to be or not to be, God and the D&RG Railroad only know. If they are in "cahoots" we ask for a special dispensation."*[22]

The proposed town of Durango was platted (laid out) in the spring of 1880 by the Durango Trust. Even before the railroads completion and arrival into Durango, the town was already growing and developing in anticipation of its arrival. From the outset, the Trust recommended that the central blocks of Durango be constructed of brick and stone.

# Durango Is Born

History had already demonstrated the dangers of building in wood. Just nine years earlier, on October 7, 1871, the Great Chicago Fire ignited. By the time it was extinguished, some four and one half square miles of Chicago had burned, consuming 17,500 buildings. Although the Great Chicago Fire is immortalized, few have knowledge of the fact that at the exact same time Chicago was burning, an even greater firestorm was occurring in Wisconsin! 16 towns in Wisconsin near Green Bay became charred cinders along with 1.25 million acres of forest, killing 1,200 people! So yes, building with brick and stone was highly recommended. Despite this recommendation, most of Durango was being built out of wood. One early resident even called the majority of the homes going up - "shacks." [23]

It seems that one of the first priorities was speed. The town was literally exploding with activity and growth! The first hotel in Durango was the "Grand Central" built by Thomas Rockwood in 1881. Even before the roof was put on, occupants were already staying in the hotel! As the photo shows, it was a wooden structure, the norm for most builders.

**The first hotel in Durango built in 1881. Before the roof was on, there were already occupants staying here. The Grand Central was located on Main Avenue at the intersection of 11th Street, on the southeast corner of the intersection. Off to the right you can see the tower of the City Hall.** *Courtesy of Roderick E. Barker*

What was Durango like in 1880? Mr. A. P. Camp reached Animas City in August of 1880. Soon after his arrival, the postmaster of Animas City asked Camp if he would like to go and see the eventual location of the new town. Mr. Camp related: *"We drove down and forded the river at the foot of what is now Cemetery Hill. The whole place was covered in sage brush, sun flowers and some lofty pine trees."* The town agent, James Luttrell walked with Camp and told him the plans. *"Main Avenue will be the wholesale street, Second Avenue—Retail Business, Third Avenue will be one hundred, twenty five feet wide, it will be a boulevard and it is to have rows of trees down the middle like Colorado Springs."* [24]

In the mean time, other preparations were underway. The Silverton Smelter at Cement Creek, built in 1874 by George Greene and Co., was purchased by the New York—San Juan Smelting

# Durango Is Born

and Mining Company in 1879. It was dismantled and moved to Durango, though not put into operation until 1881. Palmer's plans for a major development in the San Juan Valley, south of Animas City, was taking shape.

As families moved into the area, the town began to rapidly develop. The Greenfields moved from Denver to Durango in October, 1880. Their children included Elfreda and Walter. Upon their arrival, their father purchased a lot on Fifth Street for $150.00 and built a small wooden house. Within short order, the wood structure was replaced by a stone house, the first to be built in Durango. Elfreda remembers when *"on a daily basis the Indians would gallop by their house. On one occasion, upon waking up, they found that some Indians had erected their teepee right across the street in front of their neighbors' home."* [25]

Although people were arriving in Durango, purchasing property from the Durango Trust and erecting "shacks" and businesses, they were doing so without any protection from the law or even a town government! *The Durango Record* of March 12, 1881 detailed the expanding growth, stating:

*"The population of Durango is approximately 2,500. There are 150 business houses, including 6 dry goods stores, 3 drug stores, 1 bank, 1 smelter, 5 lumber companies, 10 real estate firms, 6 hotels, 10 restaurants, 4 meat markets, 20 saloons, 1 variety theater and 2 newspapers."* [26]

This small town had popped up but no government would even be elected until May 13, 1881, when the first mayor, Mr. John Taylor would be elected. Because of this, Durango, especially in its opening years, was an extremely rough town to live in.

*"Mrs. Balsey Kern arrived in Durango in August of 1881 to meet her husband who was already in Durango. She arrived with her young son and daughter. Upon her arrival she became frightened because of the wilderness of the territory, the Indians and the shooting cowboys and wanted to get right back on the train the very next morning and head right back to Denver. When she laid her eyes on the tent-house that Mr. Kern had prepared for her, the desire to leave was intensified."* [27]

*"Mr. Kern recalled seeing frozen bodies that had been recovered from snow slides standing against the wall of the undertaking establishment to thaw out. He considered Durango to be a terribly tough place; there were Red Light Districts, much drinking and gambling, shooting cowboys and hangings. Men were hung on a big pine tree that stood at Main Avenue and Ninth Street."* [28] *(Note photo on following page.)*

*The Durango Record* was the first newspaper in Durango. Starting in a tent, the first published newspaper was owned, edited and published by a woman, a Mrs. C. W. Romney and was first printed on January 10, 1881. For a woman to own and operate a newspaper in the wild West, you had to be a very special person with a strong personality. Mrs. Romney certainly filled the bill. She wrote:

*"There is probably not a man in Durango who does not carry on his person a double action six-shooting revolver. When they congregate every night at the various resorts, it is a matter to be wondered at that there is so little bloodshed. Western men value their lives little more than they do those of others, and are ready on suitable occasion to risk them. While the*

# Durango Is Born

*Durango in 1881 looking west toward the Animas River at the intersection of G (9th) Street and Main Avenue. The "Hanging Tree" is just left of center on Main Avenue.*                    Courtesy of Roderick E. Barker

*bands are playing and games are running, and everything is apparently in a peaceful attitude, parties may meet who have been looking for each other, with the tacit understanding of shooting on sight, and they shoot! The games are suspended, the music ceases, the dead and the wounded are roughly cared for, congratulations are indulged in that the deceased died "game" and with his boots on, and the carnival goes on." The Durango Record No. 8, Feb 26, 1881* [29]

Among the shortages that new towns out west often experienced was girls! Well, Mrs. Romney was going to take care of this, and she did so in a way that only she would! She ran an article entitled: *"Wanted In Durango"* She wrote:

*"We Want Girls! Girls who can get themselves up in good shape to go to a dance. The boys are getting tired of receiving invitations with a request that they "bring ladies". They are like oranges and apples, very scarce. We want girls who will go to church and to Bible class on Sundays, the kind who can draw a congregation of the other sex, and who will take a buggy ride after the lesson is over. They will help the livery business, and will also hasten the sale of residence lots for buggies are the vehicles in which homes are first thought of by many people."*

*"We want girls for sweethearts, so that when we get an arm shot off, or are kicked by a mule, or thrown from a bucking horse and are laid away for repairs, we may hear a gentle voice and see the glitter of a crystal tear, spoken in an unconscious sympathy for pain. We want fat and funny girls to make us smile all over, and lean and fragile ones to hang on our arms, and petite blondes who show themselves on sunny days; and stately brunettes, so beautiful in the twilight."*

*"We have mineral enough, and plenty of coal, and oxide of iron. The only lack of our resources is those potent civilizers of their pioneer brothers—the girls."* [30]

*Durango Record No 10 - Mar. 12, 1881*

34

# Durango Is Born

The paper went out and the girls came to Durango. One reply came from Miss M. R. Porter. She wrote: *"Noticing an article clipped from your paper - "A Cry for More Girls"- and feeling interested in the appeal, I will write a few lines to secure information. We are living here in a place where there are five females to one of the opposite sex, and there are numbers of good and respectable girls who would come to your relief, providing that positions could be found for them, where they might earn an honest livelihood. Hoping to receive some information on the subject, I will ask this question: Could there be found employment for an immigration of one hundred girls? ........If so, I will head volunteers."* [31]

Most of this excitement and action already recorded occurred before the first train even pulled into Durango! The tracks didn't reach Durango until July 30, 1881. In the *Durango Record, No 30* dated July 31, 1881 it recorded the excitement of the previous day:

*"The track reached the corporate limits about 11 a. m. and when at 5:00 in the evening, the construction train reached G Street (Now Ninth Street) in about the center of the city, the enthusiasm could no longer be restrained. Men, women and children lined Railroad Street for nearly its whole length; sidewalks, doorways, and windows were crowded; the members of the City Band assembled at the corner of G Street and commenced playing lively airs, and this of course brought out everybody."*

*"Soon the officers of the City Government appeared on the scene, in a body headed by the Mayor with a silver spike and a hammer in the hand.... When all were assembled, our worthy townsman J. L. Pennington, with his tall figure and commanding presence, and with a claw bar extracted the iron spike inserted by the railroad men, when Mayor Taylor, spike nail in hand, inserted a silver spike made from La Plata County Ore, and with three terrific blows drove the spike clean in, thereby uniting Durango by a steel band with the civilized world."* [32]

The first passenger train to pull into Durango occurred 6 days after the completion of the tracks on August 5th, 1881. One of the passengers on that first train was Eva Pearson along with her mother. Eva remembered the trip well and is on record saying that:

*"When the train pulled into Durango, and we stepped off into the sage brush, for there was no station, my mother looked dazedly at my father and exclaimed "Is This Durango?"* [33]

By the end of 1881, the population of Durango had already grown to well over 2,500 residents. It was on par to becoming the second largest city in Colorado, second only to Denver. This is the town that the Strater brothers, Frank, Fred and Henry came to call their home. They had come from Cleveland Ohio in 1880 or 81. It was a totally different reality from their upbringing back East. But they came to love it as did the majority that moved here. The excitement and potential of this fledgling town was boiling over. We will devote much of the next chapter to the Strater family and their contribution toward the development of Durango.

Durango's first City Hall was built early on in the opening years of the town, perhaps 1881 or 1882. The photo on the following page was taken sometime between 1883 and 1887. The City Hall was located just east of the alley on H (10th) street, just east of Main Avenue. (When Durango was originally laid out, 10th Street was named H Street.) The second photograph on the next page shows the City Hall in its relative position with the buildings around it. Note its position toward the lower right of the photo.

# Durango Is Born

*Durango's Original City Hall located on 10th Street just east of Main Avenue Circa 1883*
*Courtesy La Plata County Historical Society*

*The large building center left with the window awnings is located at the corner of Ninth St. and Main Ave. Built in 1883, the Denver & Rio Grande's land development company was housed in this building (863-871 Main). It was built to be a model for future construction, as the Denver & Rio Grande tried to require property owners to use brick and stone in construction. Unfortunately, they were unsuccessful in this attempt, and in 1889 much of the city burned. The two story City Hall with its bell tower (Note arrow) is located directly behind the building located at the lower right side of the photo.* Courtesy of Roderick E. Barker

# Durango Is Born

*The Longfellow Schoolhouse opened in 1882. Located in the 900 Block of Fifth Avenue in Durango, this building escaped the fire of 1889 only to suffer a fate of its own fire in 1901. This building held all grades of students from 1st through 12th. Based upon the attire and the number of flags in the photo, the event taking place may be either Decoration Day (Memorial Day) or a 4th of July celebration.*

*Courtesy of Carol Strater*

## The Longfellow School

The Longfellow School that was located in the 900 block of Fifth Avenue opened in September of 1882. Professor Fox was the first Principal; he and Mrs. Sarah Scott Trew taught the 6th, 7th and 8th grades. There were no high school grades until a few years later when an addition of two more rooms was added to the building. Elfreda and Walter Harris were among the first students to attend this school back when it opened. Elfreda related in her recorded interview that *"One year an Indian mound was discovered about two hundred feet from the school yard. The excavating craze took possession of the pupils and all our spare time was spent digging in this mound, from which we took bones, pottery, and arrow heads and a small image."* She went on to say that they went further out onto the mesa and found other mounds.[34]

**DURANGO HAS DESTRUCTIVE FIRE**

**Longfellow School Gutted. Causing a Total Loss—Insurance is $9,000.**

About 11 o'clock today fire was discovered in the Longfellow school at Durango and when it was under control two hours later the school building was gutted, and though the walls still stand the building is a wreck The fire is said to have started from a defective chimney where it went through the ceiling between the second story and the roof. The building carried $9,000 insurance. The building was one of the first modern school structures built in Durango and cost between $15,000 and $20,000.

*Telluride Daily Journal  Saturday, Dec. 21, 1901*

View of Durango

taken *(Circa)* 1883 looking west, southwest.

# Durango Is Born

Strater Bros. Paints & Oils

*Above—Overlooking Durango in 1883 from the site of present day Fort Lewis College. Within a few years, the majority of these buildings would be reduced to ashes in the great fire 1889.* *Courtesy of Roderick E. Barker*

*Below—The same view 126 years later, July 2009. The original Strater Bros. Paints & Oils Store (above) along with the Strater Hotel (below) are marked as reference points.*

Strater Hotel

# Durango Is Born

*Main Avenue looking south at the intersection of Ninth Street, Cisterns were being dug at the intersections starting from Seventh Street on up  (Photo taken in 1884)*          Courtesy of 1st National Bank, Durango
                                                                                         Photo By R. B. Collins

The date November 11, 1885 certainly holds a "bright spot" in the history of Durango! It was on this date that a group of Durango citizens organized the Durango Light and Power Company which delivered the first electric service to the town early in 1887. Home and business owners in Durango had the option of electricity from dusk to 10 p.m., to midnight, or all night. Durango's first power station was a small steam plant east of the railroad tracks on 7th Street. It was the first steam powered Alternating Current (AC) power plant built in the World!

## Fire Destroys Much of Durango

July 1st, 1889 proved to be a fateful day for Durango. On that day a fire started on Main Avenue near 10th Street.  Frances Keegan Heffernan who was  living in Durango at the time, vividly recalled the day. She said:

*"The day was windy and I recall the fire brands flying from street to alley and onto the next street. From Main they jumped over to Second and then to Third Avenue and both the Methodist and Presbyterian Churches were burned."* [35]

The 1883 photo of Durango on pages 38 and 39 includes the 2 churches Frances Heffernan was speaking about. The Presbyterian Church is the church toward the lower right of page 39 and the Methodist Church is on the same street, over toward the left edge of the same page. This photo was taken about 6 years before the fire. Without a doubt the empty lots between the churches and the center of town had been filled in by the time of the fire in 1889.

# Durango Is Born

Mrs. Heffernan called it *"a terrific fire that burned many blocks in the heart of the little city"* and also said that she *"had never since seen a fire that burned so fiercely."* [36] She stated that she was *"allowed to go to the top of the hill above the Fassbinder bridge to watch."*

The fire destroyed much of the downtown district. The majority of the wood buildings that had been built were reduced to ashes. Although the City Hall was made of brick and stone, being in such close proximity to the start of the fire (one block away), it was also destroyed.

Ironically, just prior to the fire, the city had purchased a new "Silsby Steam Pumper" for fighting fires and it was kept, of all places, at the City Hall. The fire spread so quickly, that the volunteer fire fighters of Durango couldn't get to the City Hall in time to remove it from the burning building. Elfreda Greenfield Harris who had moved to Durango with her family in 1880 is quoted as saying: *"So rapidly did the fire spread that the firemen failed to get out the shining new $500 fire engine. Within an hour it was a blackened ruin."* [37]

**Photo of a Silsby Steam Pumper**

The fire destroyed much of the town, but it didn't snuff out the spirit of Durango's citizens. The town was quickly rebuilt with brick and stone. Because of this, many of the rebuilt structures exist to this day, 120 years later.

*This rare photo of Durango was taken shortly before the fire of July 1889. Taken from the Strater Hotel, the photographer preserved the view of Main Avenue north of Seventh Street. The majority of these buildings were destroyed by the fire. The Strater Hotel was not damaged by the terrible event.*

*Courtesy of Roderick E. Barker*
*Photo by R.B. Collins*

# Durango Is Born

*This photo was taken shortly after the fire in Durango in July of 1889. Complete blocks in the downtown district were left in ashes. As a reference point, the large 2 story building in the center to the right is the Longfellow School which opened on Mar. 2nd, 1882. It was located at 9th Street and 5th Avenue. Although this fire in 1889 didn't claim the school, the school was eventually destroyed by its own fire which occurred in 1901.*

*Courtesy La Plata County Historical Society*

**The photo below of the same location was taken in July of 2009**

# DURANGO'S LOSSES BY FIRE

## The Losses Will Reach a Quarter of a Million, With Only $100,000 Insurance.

## THEY WILL NOT ACCEPT AID

## Opinions Differing as to the Origin, Many Believing it was Not Incendiary.

Special to The Chronicle.

DURANGO, July 3.—Opinions differ as to the origin of the fire of Monday afternoon, sweeping away nearly all of eight blocks between H and K streets, and from Railroad street to the Boulevard, including First and Second. Many express strong doubts of it having an incendiary origin. The wind was blowing hurricane-like and the hose was all stretched out on the sidewalk on H street to dry, having been used at the fire of D. A. C. Hall, or Reid's opera house on the Saturday night previous. Durango was never before caught in such an unguarded position. The city hall getting fired so soon after the fire started in Wagner's restaurant made it impossible to get enough hose and other apparatus for extinguishing the fire that aided by the wind the whole burned district seemed to be aflame at once.

This is the second great fire Durango has had since the town was started in the fall of 1880, when several blocks were burned between the railroad and the river, but the loss by the former fire, in the fall of 1882, was not more than one-fourth as great. The first great fire would have swept a greater portion of the city away as there was then a strong wind, had the fire department and its apparatus been in such a plight as on last Monday.

It is thought the city will not be kept under martial law longer than to-morrow. Very little of value remains in the ruins, though they have been under guard. Nearly 100 men have been pressed into martial service since Monday night.

The vaults containing the county records stood the great heat, and the records are all in excellent condition.

Those who have sufficient means are already getting ready to rebuild with brick, as it is in the fire limit.

Numerous communications asking if aid is required have been received, but it is thought it will not be necessary to accept any. A home relief committee has already secured about $1,500, which is being paid out to those who are in absolute need. About 150 families are homeless and it is estimated that nearly 200 sufferers need aid, which will be supplied at home as long as those who escaped can support the fund.

Following is a condensed report of the losses, appearing in the Denver *Republican* this morning, which does not include a number of losses of from $50 to $500:

C. H. Burton, loss $500. Mrs. Hudson, who owned the building and another one back of it, will suffer a loss of $1,500, with $500 insurance.

The court house was valued at $7,000, with insurance of $5,000.

King Chung lost his laundry and a lot of tea and Japanese goods valued at $800. No insurance.

J. F. Schutt, residence, $2,500, with no insurance. Both Mr. and Mrs. Schutt were badly burned about the head and face in trying to save some of their cherished things.

J. R. Wakelin, residence and household goods, loss $1,500; no insurance.

Smally & Hoagland, second-hand store, loss $2,500; insurance $1,200.

B. R. Elliott, damage to residence and furniture, $400.

Richard McCloud, damage to furniture, $400; no insurance.

Isaac Cherry, brick business building worth $2,000; insurance $1,700.

Henry Krumpanitzky owned the building occupied by W. L. Moore. His loss is $1,500.

M. H. Copeland, commission merchant, loss $200.

M. Stem, damage to stock, in the neighborhood of $1,500.

A. C. Meyers saved all his horses and most of his buggies. His loss will be $2,500; fully insured.

Frank Young, damage to house, furniture and clothing, $3,000; insured.

Dr. Griffith, two story residence, $1,500.

O. F. Boyle owned Noll's saloon and two other buildings. His loss is $4,000; insurance $1,200.

Boyle & McCloskey, offices fixtures, $400; insurance, $200.

Presbyterian church, loss $5,000; insurance, $4,000.

Wilder's gallery, loss $700.

The *Idea* newspaper office on Second street was totally destroyed. The material was valued at $3,000; insured at $2,500.

The Clipper theater building, owned by Charles Newman, loss $7,500; insurance $2,000. Mr. Newman also lost a house on the Boulevard worth $750, with insurance of $500.

W. L. Moore, stock valued at $3,000; insurance $2,300.

Grand Central hotel, valued at $20,000; insured at $8,000.

J. N. Galloway, loss $4,000; insured for $1,500.

M. L. Green, loss $2,000; insurance $500.

W. W. Duncan, loss $1,500; insurance $800.

D. A. Holmes, residence valued at $8,000; no insurance.

A. Bartholomew, residence valued at $2,000; insured for $1,000.

Mrs. Morelock, residence valued at $2,000; insurance $1,200.

George E. Prewitt, dwelling valued at $1,500; insurance $1,000.

A. C. Myers, dwelling valued at $1,500; insurance $1,000.

Miss Haffling, loss $500; insurance $150.

The city hall and other city buildings, $3,000 insurance. The steam fire engine was destroyed with the city hall, valued at $6,000, also 1,000 feet of hose.

Mrs. Schwartz's building and restaurant; loss $2,500, insurance $1,300.

Sherman House, valued at $7,000; no insurance.

Vandegrift & Kossman, loss $700; insured for $400.

Dr. Rader, two houses valued at $1,200, insured for $200.

I street lodging house, value $1,500, insured for $1,000.

Ana Williams, loss $2,000, no insurance.

Julius Wheeler, loss $6,000, no insurance.

W. D. Warren's store, valued at $1,200, insurance $800.

Claydon & Weinig, building and restaurant, value $2,000, insured for $600.

H. H. Strater, residence, valued at $1,500, insurance $700.

H. L. Rice, residence, occupied by his parents, value, $2,000; insurance $1,200.

The new city library, loss $3,000.

The Colorado House, value $3,000; insurance $1,000.

Frank Hoagland owned about $2,000 worth of goods; his loss is $1,400.

J. A. Boston lost $3,000; no insurance.

Joseph Clark's loss is about $15,000, partially covered by insurance.

William Valliant's saloon, $2,000; insurance $1,250.

James Barrie, second hand store on First street and house on Second street, loss $6,000; no insurance.

Ben Sherer's saloon, owned by R. H. Hutton, of Colorado Springs; valued at $2,000; stock $1,000; no insurance.

Windsor restaurant, $1,200; no insurance.

# Durango Is Born

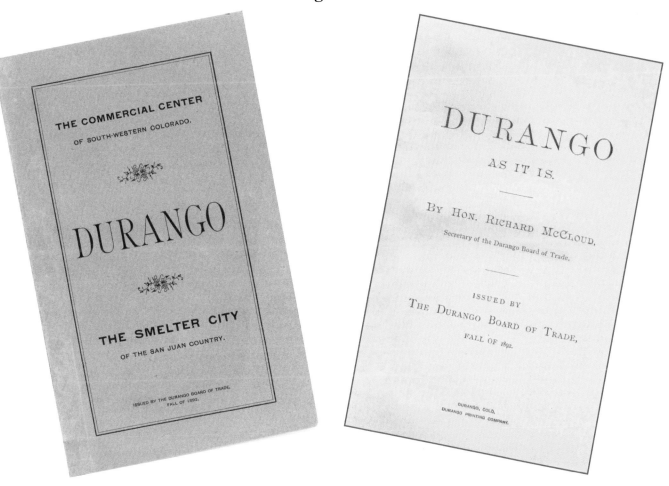

Researching among Rod Barker's historical artifacts, you can only imagine the excitement that I felt when I came upon a book in near perfect condition, dating back to the fall of 1892! The title page said it perfectly: "Durango—As It Is." Here at my fingertips were the words of Richard McCloud who was alive when Durango was still in its infancy. I was able to learn firsthand what he was seeing and feeling. I don't know for sure, but the copy that I was able to study may be the only copy left in existence today!

The rest of this chapter is word for word dictation of notes that I gleaned from the booklet, ***"Durango—The Smelter City."***

"Durango was laid out as a site for a city by Dr. W.A. Bell, now of Manitou, Hon. J. A . Porter, now of Denver, and other capitalists, in the spring of 1880, and patents were obtained from the United States government for the land on Feb. 12, 1881 and March 11, 1881. On April 9, 1881, an election was held to incorporate the town of Durango, and on April 13, 1881, County Judge Hechtman of La Plata county, gave his certificate that 412 votes were cast, of which 408 were for incorporation and four against, and that he does thereby designate Durango to belong to the class of corporations known as incorporated towns.

# Durango Is Born

The first meeting of the Mayor and Board of Trustees of the Town of Durango was held on May 16, 1881.

The census of 1885 gave Durango 2,254 and made it a city of the second class. The census of 1890 made the population 2,726; but since then (*As of the Fall of 1892*) the city has made great strides, and there are now fully 9,000 persons within the city limits.

Durango was made the county seat of La Plata county the same year it was made an incorporated town.

The San Juan and New York Smelting Company moved its plant to Durango from Silverton in 1880, because it was easier for the ores to reach Durango by a down hill grade than it was for the ore to reach Silverton by an uphill grade.

The Denver and Rio Grande railway was completed to Durango from Denver in August, 1881, and to its terminus, (*Terminus means end of the line*) at Silverton, in July, 1882.

## U.S. Land Office

The United States land office of Durango, Colorado, opened its doors to the public on October 2, 1882, and since then it has sold 102,000 acres of land, under the pre-emption laws, at $1.25 per acre, and given away for the fees, 50,000 acres of land, under the homestead laws. It has also issued over 1000 receipts for gold and silver mining claims, averaging three locations to each receiver's receipt (lodes at $5 per acre, and placers at $2.50) making about 3000 mines, (*Gold is generally found in two types of deposits: lode (vein) or placer deposits. It is usually extracted from lode deposits by drilling or blasting, whereas placer deposits require hydraulic mining, dredging, or power shoveling. Once extracted, the gold ore is pulverized to prepare it for refining.*)

## Durango Post Office

The Durango Post office opened in a cracker box on November 20, 1880, but was officially established January 3, 1881. W. M. Keightley was the first postmaster. The business of this office has increased double during the past three years. The gross receipts for the year ending Dec. 31, 1891, were $8,071.00 making it an office of the second class, and it is so recognized by the government.

## Durango—The Smelter City

Durango is called the Smelter City because God so ordained it by placing around it, on every side, coal fields of the best quality, and almost inexhaustible in quantity; also by placing close at hand lime rock and bog iron for fluxing. It is also situated geographically and so connected by railroads with the gold, silver, lead and copper mines of the San Juan country, that the ores come to the Durango smelters as naturally as the river seeks the ocean. But the smoke from the smelters does not affect the residents, as the canons and rivers form currents of air that carry the smoke away from the city.

## The Business People

(*Henry H. Strater`- a key principal in the development of Durango*) The Strater-Thorp Drug Company do a jobbing trade with $50,000.00 capital stock. Henry H. Strater is President and now have branch offices in Silverton and Rico. They intend to open stores in every principle town of the San Juan country.

In 1892 Henry H. Strater was the President of the Durango Board of Trade
He was also on:
The Finance Committee
Public Institutions and Improvement Committee
Fred W. Strater was vice president of the Colorado State Bank, established in Durango February 1887.

# Durango Is Born

## Hotels

Durango has hotel facilities surpassed by no city of 20,000 inhabitants. The Strater Hotel is the largest and best furnished. The building and furnishings cost about $70,000, and was erected by the Strater family under the management of Henry H. Strater, at a time when it was not certain whether Durango was to remain a mining camp or become a metropolis. This display of their faith gave confidence to others and in a very great measure made Durango what it is today. The Strater Hotel is run under lease by H. L. Rice. The Straters' have nearly completed a hotel building adjoining this that will cost about $50,000, that may be opened as a new hotel before January 1, 1893.

## Electric Light

Durango was one of the first cities in the state to adopt electric lighting. The company was incorporated August 5, 1885, and commenced operations January 15, 1887.

## Railroads

Durango is the natural railroad center of Southwestern Colorado. As in classic days all roads led to Rome, so in our days all railroads in Colorado are heading to Durango. The Denver and Rio Grande first came in 1881 to get our ore and coal. The Silverton Railroad was afterwards built by Otto Mears, to connect the ore houses and ore dumps of the Yankee Girl and other Red Mountain Mines with the smelter furnaces of Durango. Mr. Mears then astonished the railroad kings by his Rio Grande Southern Railroad and its marvelous earnings in transporting the carbonate silver ores from Rico, and the gold ore from Ophir, Marshall Basin and Telluride to Durango, the Smelter City. Mr. Mears name is connected with the railroad surveys made to the south and the southwest of Durango for the transportation of our coal to California, and whatever enterprise his name is connected with is sure to be successful.

## Financial Assessment of Durango—1892

County Assessor Nickell filed his assessment abstract in the county clerk's office on August 20, 1892 making the following showing:

| | |
|---|---|
| 24,214 acres of agricultural land | $246,027.00 |
| 36,328 acres of grazing land | $45,408.00 |
| 3,856 acres of coal land | $43,632.00 |
| 98 miles of railroad and railroad property | $408,664.00 |
| 87.5 miles of telegraph and telephone lines | $3,782.00 |
| 2,331 horses | $58,600.00 |
| 141 mules | $5,280.00 |
| 91 asses | $376.00 |
| 6,784 cattle | $56,183.00 |

This with other property, made the grand total valuation of La Plata county $2,264,428. His assessment of Durango Town lots and buildings is $1,149,211.

This concludes the information gleaned from *"Durango, The Smelter City"* published in 1892 and written by the Honorable Richard McCloud.

# Durango Is Born

*Main Avenue, circa 1900. Note the Colorado State Bank on the corner. This bank was established in Durango in February of 1887. Fred W. Strater, the brother of Henry who built the Strater Hotel, was vice president of the Colorado State Bank in 1892.*

*Courtesy La Plata County Historical Society*

From the records of 1892 just presented, did you note the frequency and the importance of the Straters in the town's activities and functions? It stated that Henry H. Strater was the President of the Durango Board of Trade; he was also on: The Finance Committee and Public Institutions and Improvement Committee. We also note that Fred W. Strater was vice-president of the Colorado State Bank.

McCloud stated that because of Henry Strater, Durango had some of the best Hotel facilities in the country. He said that the *"Strater Hotel is the largest and best furnished. The building and furnishings cost about $70,000, and was erected by the Strater family under the management of Henry H. Strater, at a time when it was not certain whether Durango was to remain a mining camp or become a metropolis. This display of their faith gave confidence to others and in a very great measure made Durango what it is today."* What a tribute to the contributions of Henry Strater and the Strater family as a whole!

Who was Henry Strater? What do we know of his family? For that matter, what was it like to come to the Strater Hotel in the 1880's? What was his background and what ever became of Henry Strater? These are all questions begging for an answer. We will attempt to delve into these questions in the next chapter.

# Chapter Three
## 3

# Henry Strater and the Strater Hotel
# 1880 - 1895

# Henry Strater and the Strater Hotel   1880 - 1895

*The Strater brothers* Frank, Fred and Henry were raised in Cleveland, Ohio by their parents Anton and Mary Strater. Their father, Anton Strater was born in Westphalia, Prussia in May of 1828. He came to the United States in 1842 first locating in Boston, where he engaged at his trade, that of a coppersmith. While living in Boston, he met and courted Mary Honack. In early 1856 they married. Two of their three sons, Frank being the oldest, and Fred were born in Boston. In 1858, shortly after Fred's birth, they relocated to Cleveland Ohio. In 1859, they were blessed with a third son whom they named Henry.

Anton continued on with his trade in Cleveland and became very successful. The trade of Coppersmith included making items such as jewelry, jugs and vases, sculptures, plates and cook-ware, trays, frames, rose bowls, cigarette boxes, tobacco jars, tea and coffee pots, awnings, and stills. Many other abilities were included in the trade of a Copper-smith. Plumbing was a major feature in the trade as well. By 1872, the Strater Plumbing Company had been established and was advertised in the 1872 Cleveland Directory as A. F. & H. Strater Company at 90 Erie Street, Cleveland, OH.

*Anton Strater 1828—1894*

*(Left to right) Fred, Mary, Henry and Frank Strater circa 1863*

Anton's oldest son Frank was working in the trade with his father at an early age. According to the "Cleveland Leader" Newspaper dated August 2, 1872, the Strater Plumbing Company had been doing much of the work for the booming oil refiners in Cleveland. Young Frank and a fellow worker had been dispatched to repair a leak in a large oil tank on Thursday, August 1st, 1872. While working on this tank, an explosion occurred that killed the fellow worker instantly and also nearly killed Frank. Thankfully for the Straters, Frank recovered from his injuries.

Anton's skills and abilities were many. Evidently, he also worked to some degree with John D. Rockefeller and is credited with assisting Rockefeller in the gasoline cracking facilities. "Cracking" is the process of heating crude oil to very high temperatures, providing enough energy to break

*Henry, Fred and Frank Strater circa 1866*
*Photos Courtesy of Carol Strater*

down the crude oil, and distill it into gasoline.   This is the process by which gasoline is produced to this day.

By 1880, all three sons had grown up to be fine young men. Frank was 24, already married to his wife Emile, and had two of their five sons. Fred was 22 and Henry 21. Sometime between 1880 and early 1881, the Strater brothers decided to move to the new town of Durango that was sprouting in Colorado.

*(Left to right) Frank, Henry and Fred Strater circa 1879*
*Courtesy of Carol Strater*

The Strater brothers started their journey from Cleveland to Durango by railroad. It's possible that they traveled from Cleveland to Chicago, and then from Chicago to Denver. Somewhere between Denver and Durango, the railroad came to an end.

The railroad didn't reach Durango until August of 1881, so they had to have come a good distance either on horseback or by horse drawn wagon.

Interviews with Frank Strater's grandchildren Betty Strater Albrecht (82), Carol Strater (72) and Rita Strater (66), revealed that the Strater Plumbing firm in Cleveland had bid on and was awarded the plumbing contract for the town of Durango back at its infancy. Their job would be to bring the water in from the river to the town. This might have been their original motive for making this journey back in 1880.

The Strater Brothers were not limited in ability to just the plumbing business. Within months of their arrival in Durango, they established the Strater Brothers Paints and Oils Store. Although the eldest son Frank was the one that made plumbing his primary vocation, Fred and Henry ventured out into other activities. We know that Henry, the youngest of the three was a pharmacist. Fred at some point, became involved in banking. They remind me of Otto Mears in that they were not afraid to take on any task that came their way.

By 1881, the Straters had purchased a number of lots throughout Durango. Aside from their residences, they also purchased a number of prime commercial properties on Main Avenue. The first structure to go up was the Strater Bros. Paints and Oils Store. Built by 1881, the original structure was a small one story brick building. Because of the details in the following photo, including the train in the background and the clothing, we can determine that this photo was shot after the arrival of the train in the 1st week of August, and prior to the winter of 1881.

With the town booming as it was in those early years, there is no doubt that this store was a huge success. In fact, by 1882, the Straters were more than doubling the size by extending the back of the building and also adding a second level. The next photo provides us with the accuracy of this date.

*The original Strater Bros. Paints and Oils Store in 1881*

The lower photo was taken on June 23, 1882 between the hours of 9:00 and 10:00 a.m. This is a photo of the only legal hanging ever to take place in Durango. George N. Woods was being executed for cold blooded murder of an unarmed defenseless citizen, a Mr. M. C. Buchanan. There were about 300 men, women and children on hand to watch him hang. The hanging took place at 10:00 a.m., one month to the day after his crime.

What makes this photo so invaluable to the Strater Hotel Story, is that the building under construction just behind the gallows is the Strater Brothers Paints and Oils Store! I discovered this photo while visiting the Strater family back in Cleveland, Ohio in the spring of 2009. Up until then, they had no idea of what this photo was. It was among the photos that had originally belonged to their grandfather Frank, one of the three Strater brothers making the journey to Durango back in 1880.

*June 23, 1882, the only legal hanging on record in Durango is about to take place. The Strater Bros. Paints & Oils Store is directly behind the gallows.*                    *Photos Courtesy of Carol Strater*

# Henry Strater and the Strater Hotel   1880 - 1895

**The completed 2 Story Strater Bros. Paints and Oils Store-1882**

*Courtesy of Roderick E. Barker*

When I first viewed this photo and recognized the building, I was simply elated! This was a time capsule with a positive date identification. What a treasure to find! Compare this to the photo above displaying the completed store. Do you see the distinction in the mortar of the brick toward the front on the second level? It matches the outline of the photo on the previous page. The fascia was added last. This is the reason for the difference in mortar.

Heeding the admonition to build with brick, the Straters had a structure that was highly regarded in town. Within a brief number of years, the use of this building experienced a number of changes. Marion Jarvis's original booklet entitled *The Strater Hotel Story* spoke of architect's drawings showing the floor plan for Durango's Court House in this building. The drawings included vaults which were placed on both levels. A brick building was definitely more secure than wood!

A number of years passed by. A grand hotel was a dream in the mind of Henry H. Strater. He had his heart set on building the largest and finest hotel in the West. It would be quite a challenge, because he didn't have the money nor the experience in the hostelry business. However, he did have the insight to appreciate the financial capability of a first class hotel. Hotels in the 1800's served as signs of prosperity and as symbols of a community's "class" and its arrival on the urban scene.[38]

Visitors coming into town after weeks or even months on the dusty trail, or after a long and exhausting journey by train, longed for a "homelike" meal and "sheets, pillows and coverlets to rest their weary souls."[39] During a town's rush and early boom days, few businesses proved

# Henry Strater and the Strater Hotel   1880 - 1895

**Henry Strater**

more lucrative than the hotel business. Rooms of any kind, let alone decent ones, came at a premium. Henry's intention was to tap into this booming industry.

Durango already had a number of hotels that had popped up. Laura Byrne, the wife of a doctor at Fort Lewis, stayed at the Grand Central which was one of the best hotels available in the community in 1881. Rather than getting a restful nights sleep, she stated that *"every sound drifted through the thin board partitions. Laughter, voices, the clink of billiard balls, even the rattle of poker chips disturbed her sleep until well into the early morning hours."* [40]

By late January 1881 with Durango only five months old, it was already *advertising the Delmonico, European, Windsor and Grand Central Hotels. Within six more weeks, the number had jumped to six.* [41]

Henry was witnessing this develop. His intention was not to follow the example of his predecessors. He had the ambition and desire as well as the property to build. The lot next to the two story Strater Brothers' Paints and Oils store belonged to him.

Henry convinced his father Anton, back in Cleveland, to invest the family fortune in a new hotel in the West. Henry borrowed the money and, with the help of relatives and a lot of enthusiasm, his dream became a realty.

A crew of 20 men worked into the late hours each night in the fall of 1887 and by the time the new year rolled around, this structure began to present a *"very pretty appearance as it became more and more apparent that it would be one of the finest structures in the state."* [42]

The Strater House was completed at a cost of $70,000, an extravagant figure for the time. To help put this amount in perspective; In 1887, a farm laborer was earning $1.38 per day; a painter $2.93 per day; a bricklayer $2.94; a carpenter $2.24 and a plumber $3.52 per day. Non-farm employees in the U.S. made $509 annually. [43]

In comparison with wages today; To undertake an ambition of similar magnitude today would be comparable to a current day person who is making $50,000 per year, getting loans to build a hotel that would cost 140 times his annual earnings, - $7 million dollars! Without a doubt, Henry had big dreams and big ideals.

The Strater was constructed of 376,000 native red bricks with hand carved sandstone cornices and sills. At the time of construction, bricks cost $4.50 per thousand. The bricks alone amounted to $1,692 dollars, more than 3 years the average annual wage in the country at the time. The Hotel was built and it was a site to behold! Henry's dream of building one of the

# Henry Strater and the Strater Hotel   1880 - 1895

*The sandstone cornices used in the construction of the Strater Hotel, came from this quarry, located but a short distance from Durango. The woman standing, holding the open umbrella is Carrie Strater, Henry's wife. The woman sitting down is Carrie's sister-in-law Emile, Frank Strater's wife. The two young boys are Frank and Emile's sons, Frank and Herman.  Circa 1887*        *Courtesy of Carol Strater*

largest and finest hotels in the West had become a reality. Henry furnished the 50 room hotel with "comfortable" enameled steel furniture and wood burning stoves in each room. Some of the finer rooms even had pianos! Each room had a commode holding a washbowl and water pitcher. In the compartment underneath was the "facility" which was emptied each morning by the maids. The Strater was truly a modern first class hotel for the time.

It was Henry Strater's vision from the outset, for further development of the hotel in the years to come. While researching historical data at the Animas Historical Society, I came across a piece of paper that had notes written on it taken from the Durango Herald, dated Friday, December 24, 1887. I have put together a mock up of the paper on the next page, containing word for word, the information on the notes found at the museum. This identifies Henry's eventual plans to build onto the hotel that he was just about to open.

The official grand opening of the Strater House was August 31st, 1888. The newspaper advertisement in the Durango \ Morning Herald on Friday, August 31, 1888 by Henry Strater, announced that the "Strater House" was now open for reception of guests. Henry used the center of the entire page for the advertisement! He did everything in a big way. *(The original advertisement was found on microfilm at the Durango Public Library and is reprinted on the next page.)*

Henry was definitely an entrepreneur, but he recognized his lack of experience in the hotel business, so he sought out and hired someone to run the Strater House. The man that he selected was Mr. Hugh L. Rice, a competent experienced hotel operator.

# DURANGO HERALD

VOL 2 No 133        DURANGO, COLORADO    FRIDAY, DECEMBER 24, 1887        FIVE CENTS

### Construction of the Strater House

The Strater House going up at the corner of Main Street and Seventh Avenue is certainly gaining the attention of the town. When completed, this Grand Hotel will have 54 large bedrooms, 7 bathrooms and various public rooms.

The estimated cost of completion including furnishings is $50,000.00.

C.A. Lemon is the Foreman of the carpenter force building the Strater House. Mr. Paul Geier is the architect and D.C. McGregor, the contractor.

The Straters, (Henry and Fred) also own the two story building south of the Hotel and plan to add a 3rd story which will add 46 more rooms to the hotel for a total of 100 rooms.

*Henry Strater used the center of the entire page in the Friday morning August 31, 1888 Durango Herald Newspaper for the advertisement.*

*He did everything in a big way.*

*(Microfilm—Durango Public Library)*

# Henry Strater and the Strater Hotel 1880 - 1895

*Photo of the "Strater House" taken just after its completion, circa 1888. Note the original Strater Bros. Paints & Oils Store building next door. By this time it housed a number of different businesses. The windows on the left read Paul Geier, Architect. He was the architect that designed the Strater. Note the Barber's Pole in the front, this was Durango's first Barber Shop. Also, note the railings in the front and the side. There were originally stairways leading downstairs that have long since been removed.*

*Courtesy La Plata County Historical Society*

Within a short time, the Strater became a focal point for social gatherings in Durango. Women would gather in the winter and play Euchre, a popular card game played with four people, widely regarded in the 19th century as the national card game. H. L. Rice entertained the children. Rice loved children and was known for having a warm heart, although he had the demeanor of a stern man. Gambling was very popular in Durango early on and the Strater House certainly had its share of entertainment in this regard. There was a big poker game going on each night in a back room of the hotel.

*The clipping is an original advertisement placed in the paper shortly after the Strater House opened. Circa 1888.*

*Courtesy La Plata County Historical Society*

The Strater Hotel also served the community as a refuge from the elements. During the months of January and February, the average night-time temperatures gets down into the single digits with average snowfall of 70 inches per season. In cold weather, many of the townspeople would close their homes and move their families down to the Strater.

# Henry Strater and the Strater Hotel   1880 - 1895

*Original Strater House Envelope   circa 1888*

*Courtesy of Roderick E. Barker*

It would seem that a perfect arrangement had been set up with the construction of the Strater by Henry and the hotel management having been handed over to Mr. Rice. Unfortunately, that was not the case. A gross misunderstanding occurred between these two gentlemen over the lease of space for a pharmacy, which Henry had failed to include in the lease. Rice was going to charge an extremely large rent, which infuriated the young pharmacist. As we have already discerned, Henry was no quitter, so he prepared his next project. Henry built yet another building on the corner of 8th Street and Main Avenue to house the Strater Drug Store. Henry, being a licensed pharmacist in the State of Colorado, sold various items including fine perfumes, fancy toiletry, stationary, drugs, medicines and chemicals, not to mention a little snake oil.

*The Strater Drug Store located at the corner of 8th and Main Avenue, circa-1890*

*Courtesy of Roderick E. Barker*

Henry was a highly successful Pharmacist. In 1891, he was elected to the position of President for the Colorado Board of Pharmacy (see page 72). His Registration Certificate for 1896 is shown above.

In 1892, Frank, Fred and Henry Strater's parents, Anton and Marie, moved from Cleveland, Ohio to join their sons out in Durango. They were in the autumn of their lives. Mary (Marie) was 60 years old and Anton 62. Activity was stirring in the Strater family.

*Early Tin Type Photos (Also known as Ferrotype) of Anton and Marie Strater - circa 1850's*
Courtesy of Carol Strater

# Henry Strater and the Strater Hotel   1880 - 1895

Henry moved forward with his original intentions of developing the hotel. However, instead of adding on to the Strater as he had initially intended back in 1887, he built a new and separate hotel adjacent to the Strater House. He converted the original Strater Bros. Paints and Oils Store into the new hotel. He did this by enlarging the structure, doubling the width of the building and adding a third level. Upon completion, the new hotel named the Columbian, was featured as having the *"best of modern conveniences"* including forced air heating. The Columbian was opened and run by C. E. Applegate and it competed directly with the Strater House next door, each laying claim as the *"only first class hotel in Durango."*

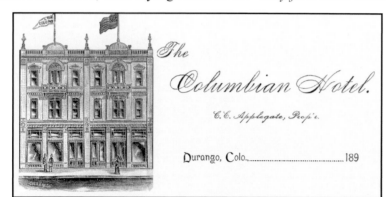

**Letterhead used by the Columbian when it opened in 1893.**

*Durango Wheel Club—Labor Day Parade—1895 posing in front of the newly constructed Columbian Hotel.*
*Courtesy of Roderick E. Barker*

60

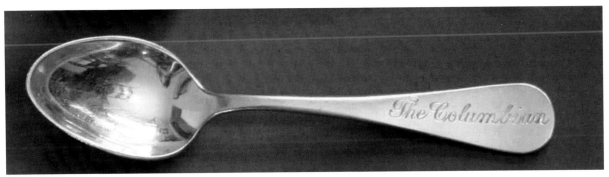

**One of the original monogrammed spoons from the Columbian Hotel.**   *Courtesy of Greg Stilwell*

**Frank Strater's newspaper ads from the 1880's.**
*Courtesy La Plata County Historical Society*

Henry's brothers Frank and Fred were also enterprising individuals. Frank Strater was busy in the plumbing industry and Fred was the Vice-President of the Colorado State Bank.

Evidently, Henry Strater in particular, played a major role in the development, as well as the success of Durango during these early years in its history. Without a doubt, he was an influential man and very much respected. In 1893, the La Plata County Circuit Judge, Mr. H. Garbanati, urged Henry Strater to run for Mayor. In a letter written to Henry, dated March 21st, 1893, he wrote: *"For the office of Mayor I know of no man in Durango who ought to make a better run than yourself, as you have in a marked degree led in enterprises that have started our city on her march to second place in the state."*

During the year of construction on the Columbian Hotel (1893), the country was entering a time of economic upheaval. Starting in 1893, the country, still on the silver standard, was finding a major devaluation of its worth. Throughout the world, except for the United States, many European nations were embracing a gold standard, and halting the mint of silver. Yet the U. S. Government, at a time when the value of silver was falling dramatically and when the nation's trading partners were abandoning silver, stepped in to promote silver against gold at the unrealistic ratio of 16 to 1! Conditions continued to worsen to the point that, by 1895, the 371¼ grain Silver Dollar was only worth 50 cents![44]

The confidence of foreigners in the American economy was also undermined. European investors expected devaluation of the dollar at the least, with complete financial collapse predicted by some. Capital flowed out of the country as overseas investors sold American securities. Even Americans began exporting funds for investment in Canada, Europe, and some of the Latin American countries; all of which seemed stronger than the United States.[45]

By the middle of 1893, Durango was already reeling from the effects of the silver devaluation. On August 31, 1893 the Durango Herald announced the liquidation and sale of the entire stock of the Strater Thorp Drug Company.

## MORTGAGEES SALE

Notice is hereby given that the undersigned have taken possession of the

### Strater Thorp Drug Company's Entire Stock

Of DRUGS, OILS, PAINTS, STATIONARY, SPORTINGS GOODS, GLASSWARE, BAR OUTFITTINGS and all goods of every line, and all accounts due them, under a chattel mortgage, and will proceed to sell the goods without delay, by wholesale and retail to satisfy said mortgage debt.

The sale will be conducted at the old stand of said company.          **W. T. KIRKPATRICK,**
**W. C. CHAPMAN**
**Mortgagees**

*The Durango Herald, August 31, 1893*

Henry Strater and his family were experiencing the dissolution of their investments and life's dreams. In 1894, matters went from bad to worse. On April 17, 1894, The Durango Herald announced that Harry Neer, considered to be one of the best barber's in Durango, had severed his relationship with the Strater Hotel Barbershop. Neer saw the "writing on the wall." By early June of 1894, Henry Strater experienced the worse case scenario that he could ever have imagined. He lost the Strater and the Columbian Hotels to the Bank of Cleveland in foreclosure! The hotels were shut down! His dreams and ambitions were dashed to pieces.

The Durango Herald, June 9th 1894 ran the news clip:

Events developed quickly following the closing of the hotels. Within one week of the hotel's closing and removal of furniture, the new owner of the hotels, John McBeth was on

H. L. Rice will finish moving the furniture from the Strater hotel today, which will be eight days of hard work that it has taken to move his outfit.

his way to Durango from Cleveland. The Durango Herald announced on June 16th, 1894:

*"John McBeth, the owner of the Strater Hotel, is expected to arrive in a few days. It is Mr. McBeth's intention to renovate the hotel and put in steam heat. There are two eastern parties figuring on taking hold of the place in addition to a couple from this section, making it reasonably safe to assume that the hotel will not remain closed for any great length of time."*

McBeth was seeking to reopen the hotel. H. L Rice, who had leased the hotel from Henry Strater, was evidently one of the local parties interested in leasing the property from McBeth. We know that they were in negotiations, however, weeks passed and the hotel stayed closed.

# Henry Strater and the Strater Hotel  1880 - 1895

On August 4th, 1894 the Durango Herald announced:

*"H. L. Rice and John McBeth, having failed to come to an understanding regarding the lease of the Strater, Mr. Rice is having plans perfected for a ten thousand dollar hotel building on his three lots on Second avenue and Seventh street, opposite the Durango Transfer company barns."*

Evidently, the announcement of Rice deciding to build a new hotel just one block away from the Strater, motivated McBeth to come to terms with whatever it was that Rice wanted, because on August 6th, 1894 the Durango Herald announced:

*"The Herald is pleased to announce that at a late hour Friday night, John McBeth and H. L. Rice came to an understanding regarding the Strater hotel and that papers were drawn up yesterday whereby Mr. Rice once again takes charge of the hotel and will open the same, on or before September 1st. This will be good news to the people of Durango, who have regretted very much to see this place closed."*

The Strater was closed for approximately ninety days, from the beginning of June on through the end of August. During this time period, the hotel was repaired, renovated, painted and cleaned. It reopened as planned on Saturday, September 1, 1894. The paper of that day announced the reopening, and also stated that the "Day Board" had been reduced to $7 per week.

This was a happy day for most of the residents of Durango, with the exception of the Strater family. We can only imagine what it must have been like, to see the most stately structure in town that you had not only envisioned, but also designed, built, and paid for, now in the hands of another. Henry was seriously distraught over this. Within one years time, he had gone from being at "the top of his game", in that he had just constructed the Columbian Hotel to compete against Rice in the Strater, to seeing both hotels that he had constructed lost, and Rice still there running "his" hotel!  Add this to the fact that he had already lost his pharmaceutical enterprise!

The devastating financial disaster also impacted Henry's father, Anton. He died within weeks of the hotel's reopening. The Durango Southwest and Herald obituaries blamed the depressing financial crises as one of the factors leading to his illness and eventual death. These have been reprinted on the next page:

# Henry Strater and the Strater Hotel 1880 - 1895

*The Southwest Newspaper Obituary*
*September 21, 1894*

*The Herald Newspaper Obituary*
*September 22, 1894*

It is with sadness that The Southwest announces the death of Anton Strater, who died at his home on Third Avenue this morning at 6:40.

Mr. Strater had been ill for a year past, but was not confined to his bed. During the last six weeks, however, he had failed rapidly, and his sufferings culminated in death this morning, Bright's disease being the case.

Mr. Strater was born in Westphalia, Prussia, in May, 1828, and came to the United States in 1842, first locating in Boston, where he was engaged at his trade, that of a coppersmith. In 1856 during his residence in Boston, he married Mary Honack, and in 1858 moved to Cleveland, O. residing there continuously until 1892, the year of his arrival in Durango.

He accumulated a considerable fortune in Cleveland, most of which was invested in Durango property, notably the Strater and Columbian hotels and houses in different parts of town.

His investments here proved unfortunate and resulted in the loss of nearly all of his money. The shock of his losses no doubt hastened his death. Three sons, Frank A., Frederick W. and Henry H. and his wife survive him.

Mr. Strater made many warm friends during his residence in Durango, who with The Southwest, extend their heartfelt sympathy to the bereaved wife and family. The body will be prepared for shipment today and will be sent to Cleveland for burial, starting on tomorrow morning's train.

At 6:40 yesterday morning, just as the sun was peeping over the horizon, the light went out in the soul of Anton Strater, the direct cause being Bright's disease although the deceased has been verly poorly the past year, and especially the last few months. Mr. Strater was born in Westphalia, Prussia, in May, 1828, and came to the United States in 1842, first locating in Boston, where he was engaged at his trade, that of a coppersmith. In 1856 during his residence in Boston, he married Mary Honack, and in 1858 moved to Cleveland, O. residing there continuously until 1892, the year of his arrival in Durango. During his residence in Cleveland he accumulated a comfortable fortune which he invested in Durango property and becoming involved was unable to save it when the panic came a year ago. This had a depressing affect on him and his old time vigor and will became dormant, although he was able to live comfortable and suffer for none of the necessities of this world's goods. He was the father of Henry H., Frederick W., and Frank A. Strater of this city, the latter two being in the city at the present time while Henry is in the East. The body will be shipped to Cleveland this morning for burial.

The Herald and a large circle of friends and acquaintances extend sympathy to the widow and the sons who miss the father who was always true and faithful to them.

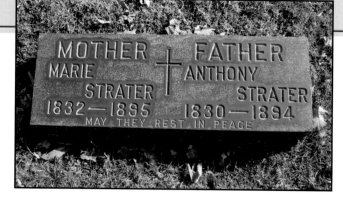

64

# Henry Strater and the Strater Hotel  1880 - 1895

Henry must have been grief stricken over the events that turned his life upside down. He might have felt responsible for his father's death. With all these factors before him, he decided that he no longer wanted to stay in Durango. This was a very difficult decision to make. His brothers and all his friends were there. Moving meant that his wife Carrie, who was well known and loved in Durango, must sever all her friendships as well. Keep in mind that she had been playing the piano in the Strater Opera House for some time. She came to be appreciated for the enjoyment that she had brought to the guests as well as the townsfolk. Before the issues with the Silver Panic erupted in 1893 and 1894, Carrie had been nicknamed "the queen" because she had the "cushy job" of entertaining, while Emile (Frank Strater's wife) her sister-in-law, had the chore of fetching water from the river in buckets for the hotel.

At least Henry and Carrie didn't have children who would be uprooted from their friends. I should clarify this, they had no living children. They should have had the joy of raising two sons. Unfortunately, one child was stillborn and the other baby died within hours of birth.

With these events compounded, it's clear to see that Henry Strater had more than his share of heartaches to deal with.

Research shows that by 1898 Henry and Carrie were residing in Philadelphia. We also have records indicating that he was on a business venture in Bolivia in 1898. Henry along with his wife Carrie, eventually moved out of the country, relocating in Cuba. Henry, the enterprising man that he was, became involved with tobacco and sugar cane along with his nephew Frank. Unfortunately for Henry, Carrie and Frank, their good intentions did not materialize. It seems that timing is everything. Just as the timing in Durango proved disastrous because of the Silver Panic, so also their decision to go to Cuba proved to be poorly timed. This was no fault of the Straters, it was just a matter of timing and unforeseen events. During the 1890's, Cuba which had been under the domain of Spain, rebelled, seeking independence. War erupted in 1895. In 1898, the United States entered the war against Spain. This war was thus named the Spanish-Cuban-American War.

In spite of the political unrest taking place, Henry and Frank moved forward and harvested their crop of tobacco and sugar cane. The crop was on the dock in Cuba, preparing for shipment to the states. Because of national developments, an embargo by the US halted all shipments. Their entire crop sat, spoiling on the dock. Distraught over these developments, they ended up dumping the entire harvest into the bay. The value was over one million dollars! By today's standards, that was equivalent to one hundred million dollars! Another fortune evaporated before his eyes!

Henry died on Dec. 9, 1914 at the age of 55. The cause of death was cirrhosis of the liver. Usually, the most common cause of this disease is over-consumption of alcohol. With the events that he had experienced in his lifetime, if that was in fact the case, we can certainly sympathize with him.

He is buried in Calvary Catholic Cemetery in Cleveland, next to his parents Anton and Marie. After his death, his wife Carrie moved back to Cleveland, and lived out the remainder of her days with Strater relatives. She is buried with Henry, in the same gravesite.

# Henry Strater and the Strater Hotel   1880 - 1895

*Henry and Carrie Strater along with their nephew Frank Strater in Cuba*

*Henry Strater in Cuba*

*Henry Strater 1905 (Circa)*

*Henry Strater's gravesite located in the Calvary
Catholic Cemetery, Cleveland Ohio.*

# Henry Strater and the Strater Hotel   1880 - 1895

The following photographs all fall into the time period of the Strater Hotel in its opening years:

*The early photo of Durango dates back to 1887—1888. The Smelter is in the foreground. The train station is in clear view as is the Strater Bros. Paints and Oils Store along with the Strater Hotel just behind it. At the time, the Strater Hotel is the tallest building in Durango. Durango is truly in it's infancy.*

*Courtesy of Roderick E. Barker*

*I climbed Smelter Mountain in 2007 in an attempt to capture the same photo as above. I ended up being a little to high and to the left. Because of an encounter with a rattlesnake, I decided against going back up for a reshoot.*

# Henry Strater and the Strater Hotel   1880 - 1895

*This photo of the Strater House was taken shortly after its completion, circa 1890.*

*Note:*
*1. The horse drawn enclosed street car to the left.*
*2. Strater Bros. Paints & Oils Store next door to the Strater House.*
*3. The Barber Shop pole in front of the store. (The first Barber shop in Durango.)*

Courtesy of Roderick E. Barker

# Henry Strater and the Strater Hotel   1880 - 1895

*Above: Early photo of the Strater Lobby Desk. Note the glass windows behind the counter. This was taken before the Columbian and the Strater were joined.*

*The safe behind the lobby counter was built in Cleveland Ohio back in the 1880's. This safe is still in use to this day, in 2009. (Note page 134)*

*Left: The original "ice machine" used at the Strater. It was located downstairs and took up a considerable amount of space. This was a fairly new invention for the time. On May 6, 1851, John Gorrie, a doctor, scientist and inventor was granted Patent No. 8080 for the first ice machine. The original model is at the Smithsonian Institute.*

# Henry Strater and the Strater Hotel   1880 - 1895

The original Strater Bar was located in the same room as the Diamond Belle today. The only difference is that the original bar was against the outer wall, whereas today, the bar is on the inner wall of the Diamond Belle. The windows are still in the same location.

*Courtesy of Greg Stilwell*

*Winter scene of the Intersection of Main Avenue and Seventh Street. circa 1898*

*Courtesy of Roderick E. Barker*

# Henry Strater and the Strater Hotel   1880 - 1895

The newspaper clippings on the following pages are the actual newspaper articles that appeared in various Colorado newspapers between 1880 and 1895 They range from humorous to tragic. The additional information has been a great aid in piecing together the early history of the Strater and also gaining information on key individuals associated with the hotel.

Mr. Henry Strater, of the firm of Strater Bro's., returned on Saturday from his trip to Rico, Ophir, San Miguel and Silverton. There is no doubt that the people of those places found Henry an oily fellow.

*The Strater brothers were well established in Durango right from its beginning in 1880. This article is humorous and was meant to be, as the Strater brothers were dealers of Paints and Oils.*

*Dolores News Sept. 17, 1881*

On Monday Mr. H. L. Rice, of the Fairplay House, sent out an order for about $100 worth of good things for the Masonic supper, such as are not in the Fairplay market. He intends to have a crack supper, and knowing well Mrs Rice's success in such matters we believe the couple will leave no reason for complaint. Tables will be laid both in the dining room and parlor for the occasion.

*H.L. Rice would eventually manage the Strater Hotel in 1888. Prior to this, he managed various hotels in Colorado. Evidently, in 1882, Rice was managing the Fairplay House. Built in 1873, it was located in Fairplay Colorado, about 23 miles from Breckenridge.*

*Fairplay Flume  Dec. 21, 1882*

# INTER OCEAN HOTEL.

## RE-MODELED and RE-FURNISHED.

## Four Squares from the Depot.

### IN THE VERY CENTRE OF BUSINESS.

The Largest Sample Rooms in Durango.

### BOARD $7.00 PER WEEK.

Stage Office for lines running to Aztec, Farmington, Fort Lewis, Mancos Bridge and the great Montezuma Valley·

## H. L. RICE. Prop'r.
**DURANGO.**                    **COLORADO**

*The Strater Hotel was under construction two blocks away from the Depot. H. L. Rice, who would become the Proprietor of the Strater within months, was running the Inter Ocean Hotel at the time, only two blocks away.*

*The Durango Herald Dec. 23, 1887*

HENRY H STRATER

*Graduate in Pharmacy.*

—Wholesale and Retail—

## DRUGGIST.

Deutscher Apotheker

—DEALER IN—

## PURE DRUGS

| ROOTS, | HERBS, | LEAVES |
| BERRIES, | FLOWERS, | SEEDS, |
| RESINS, | GUMS, | CAMPHOR, |
| BARKS, | OILS, | GLYCERINE, |
| TAR, | TURPENTINE, | HOPS, |
| BORAX, | ETC., | ETC, |

When Buying Drugs We Always Buy the Best, and Are Careful to See that they are Fresh and kept in Good Condition.

## MEDICINES !

| SWEET SPIRITS OF NITRE, | LOZENGES, |
| FLUID EXTRACTS, | SOLID EXTRACTS, |
| TROCHES, | PILLS, |
| TINCTURES, | ELIXIRS, |
| OINTMENTS, | PLASTERS, |
| ESSENCES, | CITRATES, |
| QUININE, | MORPHINE, |

AND ALL OTHER ALKALOIDS.

ALL STANDARD PROPRIETARY MEDICINES

## CHEMICALS

Brimstone, Sulphur, Copperas, Epsom, Salts, Glauber Salts. Cream Tartar, Salt Petre, Baking Soda, Sal Soda. Alum, Ammonia, Acids, Ether, Chloroform, Lunar, Caustic, Calomel, Corrosive Sublimate.

THE SALTS OF

Lime, Soda, Iron, Potash, Mercury, Lead, Silver, Zinc, Copper

### SPONGES. CHAMOIS SKIN,

Trusses, Supporters, and Shoulder Braces,

DIAMOND DYES, DYE WOOD, DYE STUFFS,

## Perfumery!

Extracts for the Handkerchief, Cologne, Bay Rum, Rose Water, Florida Water.

## TOILET AND FANCY GOODS

SUITABLE FOR WEDDING AND BIRTHDAY REMEMBRANCES, DRESSING CASES, COLOGNE BOTTLES, MANICURE SETS, ODOR CASES, BISQUE STATUARY, BRONZE STATUARY, ETC.

Hair, Tooth, Cloth, Nail and Flesh Brushes, Dress Combs, Toilet Soaps, Face Powders, Sachet Powders, Puffs, Tooth Soaps and Powders, Rouge, Hair Oils, Pomatums, Etc.

*A Complete Assortment of*

Fancy Stationery, Rubber Gloves, Bath Gloves, Turkish Bath Towels, Feather Dusters, Fishing Rods, Reels, Hooks, Lines, Sinkers, Artificial Flies and Insects, in all a full line of Fishing Tackle.

## IMPORTED and DOMESTIC WINES LIQUORS

CIGARS AND MINERAL WATER

MEERSCHAUM PIPES AND CIGAR HOLDERS.

*Henry Strater was doing quite well in the 1880's. His advertisements bespeak of his success in that he placed very large and expensive adds in local newspapers on a regular basis.*

*Durango Herald April 25, 1888*

*Into the early 1890's all was well for Henry Strater. The next news clip announces his election as President of the Colorado State Board of Pharmacy.*

The Colorado Board of Pharmacy, appointed by Governor Routt, has elected the following officers: President, H. H. Strater, of Durango; vice president, John Kochan of Denver; secretary, Thomas Axtell, of Denver. The new board enters upon the duties of office at once.

*Buena Vista Democrat, May 27, 1891*

**The following articles show a shift in business.  Note the events that began to happen starting in 1892:**

### NOTICE.

On and after August 1, 1892, I will have formed a stock drug company with H. H. Strater, of Durango, Colo., to be known as the Strater-Thorp Drug Co., operating in Durango, Silverton and Rico. All parties knowing themselves indebted to me will please make payment to Mr. Chas. E. Belt or W. F. Williams, who are authorized to collect and receipt all accounts. Parties having accounts against the undersigned will please present same before August 1.

GEO. L. THORP.

*Henry Strater and George Thorpe form the Strater-Thorpe Drug  Company.*

*Silverton Standard, August 6, 1892*

### Open All Night.

For the accommodation of the general public the Strater-Thorp drug store is now open all night. It is the only all-night drug store in the city.
4 4 tf

*The Strater-Thorpe Drug Store offered 24 Hour service over 100 years ago!*

*Great Southwest, April 12, 1893*

# Henry Strater and the Strater Hotel   1880 - 1895

The old building next to the Crystal Palace saloon was crushed in last night by the snow.

The building occupied by the Strater-Thorp Drug Company was badly crowded out of plumb by the snow.

*The Strater Thorpe Drug Store is severely damaged by the weight of the snow. The building was almost crushed. Because of this the drug store must move.*
*Silverton Standard, February 11, 1893*

Williams & Blankenburg have the contract to put in shape the store room formerly occupied by the postoffice. The Strater-Thorp Drug Company will move in there about the first.

*The Strater Thorpe Drug Store is moving into what was the post office store room.*
*Silverton Standard, March 11, 1893*

Work of repairing and straightening the building formerly occupied by the Strater-Thorp Drug Co. has commenced. As soon as it is in shape, Davis and McKinzie will move in.

*The previous store damaged by the snow is being repaired.*
*Silverton Standard, April 22, 1893*

Charley Belt went to Durango Sunday and came back the next day. He went on business connected with the drug firm. He is now a part owner in the Strater-Thorp Drug Company·

*Another partner is added to Strater Thorpe Drug Store chain.*   *Silverton Standard, May 27, 1893*

*By August 31, 1893, the Strater-Thorpe Drug Company had folded. As demonstrated through the news clips, their attempts to salvage the business proved unsuccessful. (See page 62)*

A sad accident happened in Durango on Tuesday afternoon which resulted in the death of Al. Nail. Sheriff Will T. Longnecker had left his revolver, belt and scabbard at Trimble Springs on Saturday last and his brother Ham brought them up on Tuesday. He met Will in front of the Strater House and handed them to him. Will started to put the belt on when the gun fell from the scabbard and striking the sidewalk exploded, the ball taking an upward course, and entered Al Nail's body an inch below the left nipple and came out at a point back of the left shoulder. He lived but a few minutes. He was deputy sheriff under Will Longnecker and was one of his personal friends. He leaves a wife and two children.

*A man is accidently killed on the steps of the Strater Hotel.*
*Silverton Standard  Aug 22, 1891*

A sad accident occurred in Durango on Tuesday evening of last week. While Sheriff W. T. Longnecker was buckling on his belt containing a revolver the latter dropped out and struck the stone steps of the Strater hotel. The gun exploded and the ball passed through the body of Al. Nail, a deputy, killing him almost instantly.

*Another account of the accidental death occurring on the steps of the Strater Hotel.*
*Pagosa Springs News Aug 27, 1891*

# Chapter Four
## 4

# The Strater Hotel
# 1895 - 1926

# The Strater Hotel  1895 - 1926

*The following foreword and letter* was printed in the Durango Herald Newspaper on January 3, 1896. It was written by the Mayor of Durango, A. L. Harris. Despite the issues that the town was dealing with regarding the Silver Panic, Harris was looking ahead to a very bright future. He had fore-gleams of what Durango would become in 100 years. Please note what he said:

---

**Durango In 1995**

The following was sent by Mayor Harris to the Denver Times for its New Year edition on request of the editor, but seems to have been crowded out. A comparison with what is published from Colorado mayors shows Mayor Harris to be way ahead:

**Mayors Office**
**Durango, Colo. Dec. 20, 1895**

Editor the Denver Times:

Dear Sir,

In 100 years from now all of the south half of the Pacific coast will be supplied with coal from Durango and vicinity. And the coal barons of Durango will compete with the goldbugs of its suburb, La Plata City, in giving princely entertainments.

One hundred smelters employing 500 men each will be busy night and day in smelting the ore from all over western Colorado. The silver ores from Red Mountain and Mineral Point will be dumped at the Durango smelters by pneumatic tubes.

The price of silver will be $1.50 per ounce. The palaces on Smelter hill will be connected with the city buildings on Reservoir hill by a steel bridge for foot travel and pneumatic transportation.

Statues to John A. Porter, W.A. Bell, T.C. Graden, C.M. Williams and W.C. Chapman will stand in Strater, Schutt, Kruschke, Camp, Amy and McCloud squares. Paris, London and Berlin editions of The Durango Morning Herald will be published.

The Newman block will have 10,000 rooms and be fifty stories high, surmounted by a statue of ex-Governor Charles Newman. Population 1,000,000 and extending to a radius of twenty miles.

In the summer the people of Durango can take their morning bath in the hot springs of Pagosa before going to business and labor. All of what is now the lands of the southern Ute Indian reservation will be thickly populated by Missourians, and Ignacio IV will often visit Durango from his tepee in the Blue mountains of Utah.

Yours very Truly,
A.L. Harris
Mayor of Durango

# The Strater Hotel  1895 - 1926

*This photo has special significance because it clearly shows that the Strater Bar was still in operation when this photo was taken. The picture was taken after 1898. We know that, because the Savoy Hotel (now named the General Palmer) is seen at the left edge of the photo. The Savoy hotel was not built until 1898, ten years after the Strater's Grand Opening.*

*Courtesy of the Roderick E. Barker*

# The Strater Hotel  1895 - 1926

The economic depression that began in 1893, causing the Silver Panic of 1895, brought about severe economic hardships throughout the country, as well as Europe. Durango faired no better. In fact, with its dependence on silver, it was worse off than many. Although John McBeth had taken over ownership of the Strater Hotel as well as the Columbian, the ensuing years were very difficult.

**Charles Stilwell standing in front of the Strater**
Courtesy of Greg Stilwell

The agreement that H. L. Rice and John McBeth had come to in 1894 did not last. Before long, McBeth was looking for someone qualified to take over the management of the Strater.

By 1896, the Strater Hotel was under the management of Charles E. Stilwell. Stilwell was born in Champaign County in Illinois on March 10, 1868. His family moved to Kansas after his birth. Charles left his family farm in Kansas while still in his teens to find other work. Eventually, making his way out West, he settled in Seattle, Washington. It was here that he learned the hotel and restaurant business. Stilwell eventually moved on and made his way into Colorado. He first settled in Creede in 1892. While in Creede, he found work at a saloon owned and operated by Bob Ford, the person who betrayed and assassinated Jesse James, shooting him in the back on April 3, 1882, back in Missouri.

On May 29, 1892, Bob Ford had opened a dance hall in Creede, named Ford's Exchange. Just six days later, the entire business district burned to the ground including Ford's dance hall. Within a few days, Ford opened a saloon in a makeshift tent. This is where Charles Stillwell was working on June 8th, when the infamous Edward O'Kelley walked in with a sawed off shotgun. Ford was standing with his back to the entrance about five feet away, when O'Kelley called out; "Hello, Bob." As Ford turned around coming face to face with his visitor, O'Kelley emptied both barrels, killing Ford instantly![46]

Of course, this was the end of Charlie Stilwell's employment in Creede. Having no money, he literally walked over the mountains from Creede to Silverton, some 60 miles! In Silverton, he was able to obtain transportation either by train or stagecoach down into Durango.

The next two years are unclear, but we can assume that Stilwell evidently prospered in Durango. We know that in August of 1894, he purchased the restaurant of M. L. Green. Prior to that, he had been running the Horse Shoe Restaurant. In 1896, he took over the active management of the Strater.

Hattie Mashburn was working in the Strater Hotel, managing the Housekeeping Department. Charles E. Stilwell and Hattie Mashburn at some time in these early years became partners and ran the hotel together. John Macbeth Sr. retained ownership of the properties while Stilwell

# The Strater Hotel  1895 - 1926

*Charles Stilwell and Hattie Mashburn in the Strater Hotel office in 1906.*
*Courtesy of Greg Stilwell*

ran the business. It was in 1902 that Stilwell & Co. joined the Strater and the Columbian hotels into the one Strater Hotel.

Hotel operations at the turn of the century were a vastly different experience compared to today. Stilwell's background was in the restaurant business and Mashburn was the Executive Housekeeper of the Strater. Both worked well together and the hotel recovered from the hard times of the 1890's, though not with a great profit. To make ends meet, both the hotel and Durango locals looked to each other as a matter of economic necessity. During the cold winter months, it was not uncommon for local residents to temporarily move into the hotel to save the on the cost of heating their own homes. Not only did the locals live at the hotel, so did the maids and the waitresses. Their employees quarters were all located at the back of the fourth floor of the hotel. The fourth floor also earned the nickname "Monkey Hall" because of the "monkey-shines" that were taking place. Hattie Mashburn was running a Brothel on the fourth floor! At the time, some of the walls on this floor were only made of canvas material, so there was little privacy and it was easy for "extra guests" to slip in and out.

The Strater became a popular winter retreat for travelers all over the west. Each room had its own wood burning stove, a commode, holding a washbowl and water pitcher, and in the compartment underneath was the "chamber pot", which was emptied every morning by the maids. The maids were paid $20 per month.

When the Strater was originally built, it had a total of seven bathrooms. These were really nothing more than indoor outhouses. The "bathrooms" were "strategically" designed privies built at the rear of the hotel.

Charles Stilwell is credited with improving the sanitary system of the hotel by installing the first "sewer" system in Durango. He built a square wooden sewer and buried it alongside the railroad tracks behind the Strater. He also buried wooden pipes leading directly to the Animas River. The Strater's three story privies, consisting of the "strategically" placed holes (gravity operated) and shafts were connected to the wooden sewer Stilwell had built. This way, the raw sewage could now be emptied directly into the river. At this time in history, this was "modern" technology. It was not uncommon for cities to use rivers for their sewage system.

# The Strater Hotel 1895 - 1926

There were also several bathing rooms where ported hot water was drawn by the staff at a cost of twenty-five cents ($.25). After weeks on the dusty trail, the baths were one of the best amenities a hotel could offer. Service was a valuable and appreciated amenity to hotel guests. The hotel Annunciator was a useful aid in rendering service to guests.

The Strater hotel "Annunciator" was located on the wall behind the front lobby desk. The porter could be summoned from any room by means of the Annunciator Panel. This was a one way communication system from a guest's room. The Annunciator was invented in 1829 by Seth Fuller. This device entailed a knob located in the guest room that connected to a wire which ran to a panel at the front desk. At the front desk, the panel was covered with a series of small bells and a coiled spring on each bell. When the wire was pulled at the guest room end, the spring would recoil until the guest let go, and the bell would ring. Upon the sound of the bell, the porter would rush to see which of the coiled springs was vibrating. There was no time to lose, and thus the name of the porter became the "Bellhop." The guest would first ring the bell designating the room number. The guest would then ring

*The Strater Annunciator Panel was located just behind the front desk and to the right of the window.*

the bell again to signal his wishes. One ring designated a need for a pitcher of ice water; two rings—hot water for washing; three rings-wood for the stove; four rings-extra bedding. The system brought prompt service.

Originally, the Strater hotel had a lean-to kitchen on the west side. Not having grocery stores as we do today, restaurants and kitchens had to be self sufficient. Behind the Strater kitchen was a wirefenced chicken run where the fryers and the stewers were kept for the dining room. Milk for the tables came from the cows that were gathered each morning to be taken to pasture as part of the "town herd." Each morning after milking time, cows from all over town were gathered by young boys and driven outside the city limits to graze. In the late afternoon each cow was returned to its own yard where it spent the night. The fee for the day long "cow sitting" job was one dollar per month per cow. The Strater kept three cows.

The original dining room was in the northwest corner (Today this is Room 108 and the Manager's Office). Mr. Stilwell insisted that his male guests wear a coat while eating meals in the dining room. There was great protocol in the seating of guests. Tables were numbered one, two, three and so forth. One certain group of men (uncommonly influential, of course) sat at the head table where no one else was welcome.

Musicals were a part of living in the Victorian era. Chamber music was very popular. A few areas of the hotel were set aside by the management to be used by string trios for the entertainment of the guests.

# The Strater Hotel 1895 - 1926

One end of the early dining room was separated by double doors. This area served as a writing room. It was often opened and used by musicians who entertained the guests during the Sunday dinner hour. One such duo was headed by a professor of music, a Frenchman named J. A. Doucet. His specialty was Piano and Violin. One of his pupils was an apt Spanish girl called Rosita, who played the harp. This instrument was stored in the hotel barber shop when not in use. Professor Doucet played the piano or violin and Rosita, the harp.

> Denver Music company has appointed Prof. Doucet local agent for their noted pianos. He is located next to Gonner's, where he will carry a full line of musical goods and music. He is an expert and has catered to the Durango trade before. You all know him as a musician.

*Professor Doucet was well known at the Strater and performed there regularly. He also owned a local music store.*
*Durango Democrat Newspaper 12-03-1904*

During this time period, department stores the likes of what we have today, were rare and only found in larger cities. Therefore, traveling salesmen were prevalent throughout the United States, particularly in booming towns such as Durango. The traveling salesmen were called "drummers", because they would go around "drumming" up business. The "drummers" would arrive in Durango by the train along with their trunks full of merchandise. After establishing headquarters at the Strater, they would set up their wares in one of the six basement "sample rooms" that the Strater had designated for this purpose. Here, potential customers would come to view the salesman's merchandise. Traveling salesmen proved to be a very important means of income to the Strater for many years.

*Hattie Mashburn on her bicycle in front of the Strater, circa 1903*
*Courtesy of Roderick E. Barker*

# The Strater Hotel  1895 - 1926

The first barbershop at the Strater was run by Frank Cunha and was located in the room that "The Office Spiritorium" occupies today. The chairs were beautiful examples of Victorian elegance. They were constructed of heavily figured cast iron and upholstered in Spanish leather. Dozens of shaving mugs bearing their owners' names and often a special picture illustrating the owner's job, decorated the walls.

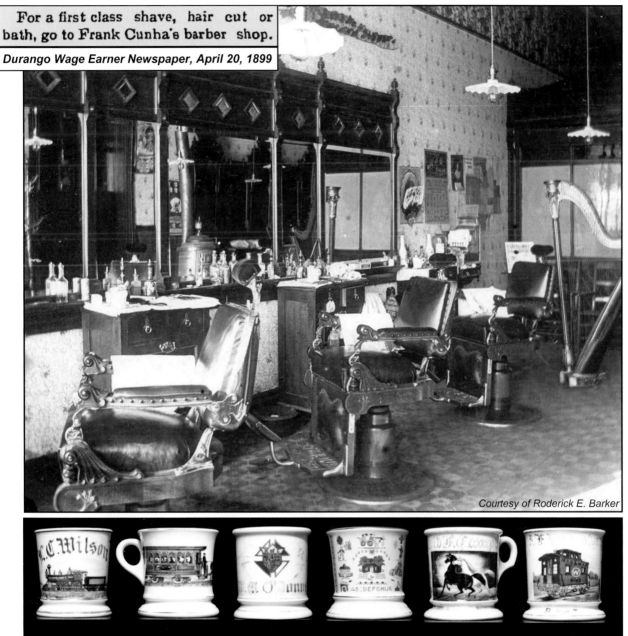

> For a first class shave, hair cut or bath, go to Frank Cunha's barber shop.
>
> *Durango Wage Earner Newspaper, April 20, 1899*

*Courtesy of Roderick E. Barker*

*Personalized shaving mugs such as these hung on the wall of the Strater Barber Shop. The mugs were manufactured in Europe and decorated in the United States. Mugs of this type were in vogue from the 1860's to the 1920's.*

*Mug Photos courtesy of Michael Burchinal*

# The Strater Hotel  1895 - 1926

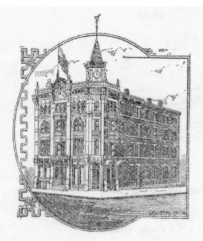

## STRATER HOUSE.

The Finest Hotel in the San Juan.

New Building and New Furniture.

. . Stilwell & Co. . .

DURANGO., COLO., ———————————— 1896.

*The Strater House stationary behind the envelope is dated 1896. In the drawing of the Strater on the stationary, note that the Columbian Hotel next door, is not shown. In 1902, Stilwell and Mashburn annexed the Columbian into the Strater Hotel. The envelope, postmarked March 04, 1904 displays the combined hotels, although they exaggerated by adding a fourth story onto the Columbian annex.*

*Courtesy of Roderick E. Barker*

# The Strater Hotel 1895 - 1926

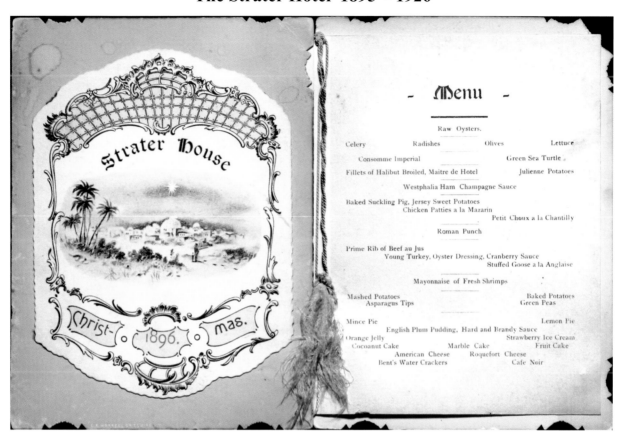

**Strater House**

Christ-mas. 1896.

**- Menu -**

Raw Oysters.

Celery  Radishes  Olives  Lettuce

Consomme Imperial    Green Sea Turtle

Fillets of Halibut Broiled, Maitre de Hotel  Julienne Potatoes

Westphalia Ham Champagne Sauce

Baked Suckling Pig, Jersey Sweet Potatoes
 Chicken Patties a la Mazarin
       Petit Choux a la Chantilly

Roman Punch

Prime Rib of Beef au Jus
 Young Turkey, Oyster Dressing, Cranberry Sauce
     Stuffed Goose a la Anglaise

Mayonnaise of Fresh Shrimps

Mashed Potatoes      Baked Potatoes
 Asparagus Tips      Green Peas

Mince Pie        Lemon Pie
 English Plum Pudding, Hard and Brandy Sauce
Orange Jelly      Strawberry Ice Cream
 Cocoanut Cake  Marble Cake  Fruit Cake
  American Cheese  Roquefort Cheese
  Bent's Water Crackers   Cafe Noir

*Top—1896 Strater Christmas Card along with a special holiday menu.*
*Below—Hattie Mashburn (right). The names of the other two ladies are not known.*

*Courtesy of Greg Stilwell*

# The Strater Hotel 1895 - 1926

As the year 1900 ushered in, no one knew of the event that was to happen within a few months that could have meant the total demise of the Strater Hotel. Business was good, and life at the Strater was normal until Thursday evening, May 24th.

One of the girls who worked as a Strater waitress, lived in one of the rooms up on the fourth floor. She was sound asleep until 9:55 p.m., when she awoke and discovered that her room was ablaze with fire. She was able to get out and run down the hall. The alarm was sounded and the Durango Fire Department quickly responded. Within minutes, the fire had engulfed the hallway and other rooms. The fire grew so rapidly that the future of the Strater and even the rest of the block hung in the balance! The actual newspaper articles detailing this event are just below.

*The Durango Democrat, Friday May 25, 1900*

## NOT ALL LOST

### Last Night's Fire Will Only Rob Durango of Her Chief Hotel For a Time.

About 5 minutes before 10 last night fire was discovered in fourth story of the Strater hotel. The fire bell sounded ominous, its tones denoting with human distinctness that it was neither a false alarm nor small fire. When the crowd surging down the avenue learned that it was the Strater— the city's pride—a prayer went up from every heart that it might be saved.

The department found the fourth story a mass of flames and smoke on the inside and it was a steady 4 hour struggle with five streams playing before brain, brawn and heroism triumphed. It was an uncertain fight until 11:30 or 12 o'clock and for a time earlier in the evening it looked as if the Strater, Columbian and entire block would be totally destroyed.

Chief Galbreath was cool and collected and throughout the trying ordeal displayed excellent judgment and he was ably assisted by his regular firemen and a number of citizens who volunteered. Among the latter may be mentioned, W.T. Vaile, Dan McLean, Arthur Ayrees, Walter Weightman, Bert Gartin, Mr. Grove, Charlie Allen, Jim Gorman, George Goodman, Henri Berry, Mr. Furguson, Sam Herr, Dick Wright, Frank Burgess, Johnny Herr and Frank Rose. These are only a few of the gallant fellows who labored and risked life and limb to save Durango's per hotel, we fail to remember the balance, but they were all there and that is the reason the Strater walls are standing this morning. At 1 o'clock the water was shut off and the fire declared out. The building is soaked from basement up and practically everything which remained in way of furniture is soaked. The walls are however intact as are also the floors and all the partition walls save those in fourth story. The roof is sagging in several places and will call for considerable repairs. The house will have to be repainted and repapered throughout but it is estimated at this hour that insurance will cover the entire damage and if such is the case the Strater will be itself once more.

About 11:30 Chief Galbreath made a daring ladder climb from the outside to the fourth story window of Dan McLain's room where he secured a number of articles of value but came nearly being overcome with smoke. He managed to reach the top of the ladder but how he got safely to the bottom is a mystery as he was practically unconscious. Bert Gartin, Arthur Evans and Mr. Grove were packed out of the building unconscious being overpowered by smoke while at their posts of self imposed duty.

Fire started in a room of the pastry cook and was caused by explosion of a coal lamp over which one of the young lady employees was heating a curling iron. The young lay's hair was badly singed and her hands and face more or less burned.

*The Telluride Daily Journal, Friday May 25, 1900*

## DESTRUCTIVE FIRE VISITS DURANGO.

### The Strater Hotel Practically Ruined—Guests Escape in Their Night Clothes.

*Special to the Daily Journal.*

DURANGO, May 25.—At 9:55 last night one of the waiter girls in the fourth story of the Strater Hotel awakened and discovered her room on fire. She ran out and gave the alarm. In five minutes the hallway and several rooms were ablaze. Many of the guests were asleep and there was a general scramble to get out, several escaping in their night clothes, carrying valises and dragging trunks.

While the fire department responded promptly, a large area of the fourth floor was in flames before water was turned on, one stream through the stairways of the house being carried up. For two hours it was a question of saving the large structure and it took three and a half hours to subdue the blaze with five streams of water.

Four persons were nearly suffocated from fighting fire and carried out of the building. Chief Galbreath had a narrow escape, being unconscious for an hour.

While the fire was confined to the fourth floor the building was scaled of plastering and everything ruined except the walls.

There is $25,000 insurance on the building and $5,000 on the furniture, which will cover the loss.

# The Strater Hotel 1895 - 1926

Thanks to the efforts of so many people, the Strater was saved and was restored to its rightful position of Durango's premier landmark. The following pages illustrate that all was well at the Strater within months.

**Strater Hotel Christmas Card produced by Stilwell and Co. dated Dec. 25, 1900**
*Courtesy of Roderick E. Barker*

# The Strater Hotel 1895 - 1926

The tasty and plentiful meals served at the Strater around the turn of the century usually included five courses. You could expect to be served soup, fish, a main entrée with vegetables and a delicious fritter of apples, corn or other fruits with a sweet sauce, salad, desert and coffee.

On special occasions, the meals were even more spectacular.
Note the 1901 New Year's Eve menu below:

*The embossed 1901 New Years Eve Dinner Menu Cover.*

**<u>*The 1901 New Years Eve Dinner included:*</u>** *Chicken Gumbo, Baked Mountain Trout, Prime Sirloin of Beef, Young Turkey-stuffed, Cranberry Sauce, Salami of Prairie Chicken A La Russe, Grenadine of Veal with Peas, Queen Fritters, Custard Sauce, Mashed Potatoes, Boiled Potatoes, Browned Sweet Potatoes, String Beans, Chicken Mayonnaise, Fresh Shrimp, Tartar Sauce, Assorted Cakes, English Plum Pudding, Brandy Sauce, American Cheese and Roquefort Cheese.*

# The Strater Hotel  1895 - 1926

*Corner of Main Avenue and Seventh Street—1906. The lot in the foreground was owned by Harry Jackson. The lot was patronized mainly by Indians who pitched their tents for days of enjoyment in the big town. The decorations on the hotel saluted a billiard tournament held in conjunction with a fireman's convention.*

*The Strater made use of the finest transportation available at the time. They had a bedecked "Tallyho" with a liveried driver which met each train and carried guests to the hotel. There was great competition among the drivers from each establishment as they pulled into the depot at train time. A white chalk line was drawn on the board walk to the south of the depot and each wagon or stagecoach had to "toe the mark:" The driver, waving his buggy whip could shout the benefits of his hotel to the top of his lungs, but he couldn't touch the luggage until the passengers had crossed the line. Here the spanking, dappled grey horses of the Strater attracted the most attention. They strained to be on their way, prancing the two blocks to the hotel, proudly carrying the guests with the luggage piled on top of the vehicle.*
**Photo circa 1900**
*Photos courtesy of Roderick E. Barker*

# The Strater Hotel 1895 - 1926

*This photo reveals the appearance of the entire lobby area in the early 1900's. The man to the right is Charles Stilwell. Stilwell & Co. managed the Strater Hotel up until 1922.* (Note the steam heat radiator installed in 1894, compared to photo on page 69 with the wood or coal burning stove.)
Courtesy of Greg Stilwell

*This is perhaps the earliest evening shot of the Strater that is known to exist. Taken around 1917, this photo reveals the thriving activity taking place within the Strater. Turner Insurance was currently occupying the corner space that is now home to the Diamond Belle Saloon. The Red Lantern Inn occupied the current location of the Mahogany Grill to the South.*
Courtesy of Roderick E. Barker

# The Strater Hotel 1895 - 1926

*Buckskin Charlie (1840-1936) came to the Strater and was photographed by the staircase. Succeeding Chief Ouray in 1880, he became the first Ute leader during the Reservation Period. He was instrumental for leading the rescue of the women and children abducted during the 1879 Meeker Massacre. He is also remembered for riding with Geronimo in Theodore Roosevelt's 1905 Inaugural parade.*

*Buckskin Charlie - Chief of the Utes is front right. This photo might date back to August, 1902. According the article just below, he was in Durango at this time .*

*Photo courtesy of Greg Stilwell*

From The Herald.
The Indians who are attending the district court are creating quite a lot of amusement for those who know how to talk to them. Someone asked Buckskin Charlie if he were a chief, and he answered that he was a chief of a ditch. When he was asked how old he was he couldnt remember how many years he had lived.

*Durango Wage Earner Newspaper*
*Aug. 14, 1902*

*Lower—Chief Ouray (Presumably) seated on the horse with Buckskin Charlie standing in front of him wearing the jacket and hat. He was well known for flashing his "badge" which can be identified in the photo.*

*Courtesy of Carol Strater*

## The Strater Hotel 1895 - 1926

*The Cow Girls on Parade for the Durango Fair & Roundup—September 24, 1919*
*Courtesy of Roderick E. Barker*

# The Strater Hotel 1895 - 1926

*This photo of the Strater was taken at the turn of the century, circa 1900-01. The Strater Bar occupied the corner at this time. The sign above the railing to the left of the Strater Hotel entrance is advertising the tailor J. P. Rasmusson who was operating his business downstairs at the Strater. The outside entrances to the downstairs, located in the front as well as the side of the hotel, no longer exist today.*

# The Strater Hotel  1895 - 1926

**Photo of Main Avenue in 1904. The Strater is in the background to the right.**

**Main Avenue in the early 1900's**

# The Strater Hotel  1895 - 1926

*The Electric Trolley in front of the Strater in the early 1900's.*

*Courtesy of Roderick E. Barker*

*The Durango Railway and Realty Company was incorporated on July 13th, 1892. The objective of this company was "to construct, maintain and operate a system of street and suburban railway in the city of Durango, its suburbs, and in the county of La Plata, and to acquire lines of street railway already constructed, and to operate such railways by horse, mule and electricity, cable or other power....." The "lines of street railway already constructed", referred to the Durango Suburban Street Railway, which operated from the railroad depot to the Animas river on Main Avenue. It was originally drawn by mules of horses. Later in the month of July, 1892, their corporate meeting notes indicate that they instructed Mr. Graden to take necessary steps to convert the line into an electric line, and to extend the road to "Brookside". Evidently this was done in short order, as a list of prices for power was established on Sept. 1, 1894. Unfortunately, this line never proved to be profitable. In fact, William A. Bell, one of the original developers and founders of Durango, literally paid out of his own pocket to keep this line running for many years.*

*This entire system was dismantled in the 1930's. The only records known listing the amount of equipment that they had, was the 1917 report, where they listed three closed passenger cars, two open passenger cars, and a snow plow.*

# The Strater Hotel 1895 - 1926

While researching the old Colorado newspapers, there were numerous articles written between 1895 and 1926 that add to the colorful history of the Strater. Here are some examples:

## HAS MORE MONEY THAN HE CAN USE.

Money-Throwing Croesus Strikes the San Juan and Is Not Properly Appreciated.

Durango Democrat.

Mr. M. Kinney, the Colorado Springs capitalist who gained notoriety a short time ago by throwing silver dollars away to see a crowd scramble for them, has been playing some very peculiar pranks in the San Juan. About ten days ago he came to Durango and registered at the Strater. He had his pockets filled with great rolls of bills, wore expensive diamonds and costly watch with heavy chain and a chunk of gold for a locket that weighed fully two ounces. He soon made a number of acquaintances, being a hale fellow well met, but they were of the lower order of hangers-on who deal out flattery to any one disposed to spend money on them. One night Mr. Kinney became "tanked" and Officer Bacon noticing his helpless condition and evident value of his jewelry, which was in danger of being stolen, locked him up in the city jail. The jewelry was taken to the Strater hotel and put in keeping of Manager Stilwell. Mr. Kinney was released the next morning and seemingly chagrined over his conduct, took the first train for Silverton without even inquiring for his property. In Silverton gold and silver and greenbacks flowed again from this man's pockets which seem to never be exhausted. He gave Sheriff Casad an order on Mr. Stilwell for his watch and rings. The sheriff was instructed to have them at the depot when yesterday morning's train came in from Silverton. Mr. Kinney was going east and didn't want to trouble himself about them. He gave Mr. Casad $25 when he started for expenses and another $5 when they met in Durango, just because he was a good fellow. It would have been an easy matter for the gentleman to have walked to the Strater and transacted his own business as the distance is short and his time ample. But he choose to pay $30 rather than walk two blocks. What a nice world this would be if all rich men were like this Mr. Kinney. How different he is from Russell Sage, who walks a mile and a half to save street car fare and borrows money from his clerks to pay for his lunches. We hope Mr. Kinney will come back to Durango. He was not appreciated while here and we are sure it was an oversight. We might ask him to build us an opera house or an electric road to Trimble Springs.

*Telluride Daily Journal, Sep. 18, 1900*

Painters and paper hangers under the direction of the Goodman Co. are effecting a pleasant change in the Strater hotel; the upper floors have been gone over with brush and paper and the force is now on the lower floor kalsomining hallways and re-papering dining, reading and waiting rooms. The entire hotel will be renovated from basement to attic and when completed the Strater will constitute the most pleasant hostelrie in the San Juan.

*Just 11 months before the hotel fire, the Strater received a major renovation.*
*Durango Democrat June 23, 1899*

94

# The Strater Hotel  1895 - 1926

## MINES OF SOUTH AMERICA.

FRANK G. CARPENTER, who is traveling in South America, writes most instructive and entertaining letters to the San Francisco Chronicle.  From one of them we re-publish a part which we think will be read with interest by all, by reason of the information it gives of the gold fields of Bolivia, and for the further reason that it tells us something about H. H. Strater and A. A. Hard, both of whom were formerly residents of Durango.

The article is particularly important because it revealed additional information pertaining to Henry Strater's life after he left Durango.
Durango Wage Earner Newspaper
Aug 4, 1898

LA PAZ (Bolivia), June 15, 1898—Bolivia and Peru are among the richest mineral regions of the world. Bolivia has produced more than $3,000,000,000 worth of silver. She now stands third among the silver-producing countries, and if what American mining prospectors here tell me is true, she bids fair to soon come to the front as a rich gold territory. I went out yesterday to watch the week's cleanup of a little placer mine which belongs to a number of Bolivians of La Paz. The diggings were on the Chuguiaguillo river, which runs by the city not two miles from where I am writing. This river has cut a gully several hundred feet deep in the side of the plateau or basin in which La Paz is situated, and above the cut a high wall of gravel extends to what is known as the Alto, far above the city. It is in this gravel that the gold is found. A score of Indians were at work digging down the hill, carrying off the gravel in wheelbarrows and dumping it into troughs or sluice boxes through which water from the river was conducted. On the bottom of the troughs were iron ladders or frames so laid that they would catch the heavier parts of gravel and gold as the water carried the dirt on into the river. There was no quicksilver used, and the miners depended entirely on the specific gravity of the gold to catch the particles as they went through. Shortly after I arrived the water was turned partially off and the gravel panned for gold. The panning was done by three Indians, who sat with their bare legs in the water on the sides of the sluices and dipped the gravel up into wooden bowls just about as big as those we use for making bread or chopping hash. The bowls are the gold washing pans of the Indians. They are called bateas, and are to be found in all the mining regions of Peru and Bolivia. The miners dipped the bowls of gravel from time to time into the water, and, mixing the gravel with their hands, caused the dirt to flow off. Now and then they picked up a handful of the gravel, and, after looking it over, cast it back into the sluice box. As they went on you could see little yellow bits of metal among the dark stones. After a while the gravel was all washed out, and in each bowl there was a little pile of gold pebbles or small nuggets. There was no gold dust, the deposits ranging from bits of pure gold the size of the head of a pin

to nuggets as big as the size of your little finger nail. One of the nuggets which I saw taken out weighed more than half an ounce, and it was worth I was told, at least $10. The total amount cleaned up was not large, but it was all of this coarse gold.

This is the character of the gold found in Bolivia. It lies in the earth, not in pockets, but distributed with great regularity through the layers of gravel of some parts of the country. Now and then large nuggets are found. These same gravel beds have been burrowed into by the Indians for more than 200 years, and out of almost the spot upon which we stood there was found, in the seventeenth century, a mass of gold which was sold for $11,260. It was sent to the museum at Madrid, where it is said one of the keepers had a dummy nugget made to imitate it and then stole the original and melted it up and sold it. While we were at the mine the skeleton of an Indian was dug up. He had probably been mining here generations ago and the earth had caved in and buried him.

I was sent out to this mine with H. H. Strater of Philadelphia and Professor A. A. Hard of Denver. Professor Hard is a well-known mining engineer, and he has been brought here by Mr. Strater in connection with some Philadelphia capitalists, who have taken up a large placer claim on the Palka river, about thirty miles from La Paz, at the foot of the great Illimani mountain. They have tested the property thoroughly and it promises to be one of the great placer mines of the world. The best hydraulic machinery for its development has already been ordered from San Francisco, and within a few months they will begin active work. The machinery is all made in sections, no piece weighing more than 150 pounds, as it must go to the mines on the backs of mules. Professor Hard has traveled extensively over this part of the Bolivian mining regions. He tells me there is no doubt but that there is a great deal of gold here. Said he to me today:

95

# The Strater Hotel 1895 - 1926

THE DURANGO DEMOCRAT, FRIDAY MORNING, SEPT. 27, 1901.

## New Strater Rules.

Charley Stilwell has never been satisfied with regulation hotel rules, and the following regulations were codified while he was laying awake nights:

1.—The motto of this hotel is, eat, drink and be merry when your bill is presented, but don't get gay.

2.—Travellers without trunks will be fastened to the bedpost with a chain.

3.—The elevator in this hotel has been running for four years and must now be about 41141 miles away. Those who prefer to fall down stairs do so at their own risk.

4.—There are three departments, upstairs, downstairs and outdoors. Outdoors is the cheapest.

5.—If the bell in your room is broken, wring the towel.

6.—Guests who walk in their sleep should sleep with their boots on, as tacks are strewn on the fourth floor to make painful the path of the unrighteous.

7.—The proprietor absolutely refuses to furnish alarm clocks They might go off without setting. Before retiring wind up your bed and hear the tick.

8.—Guests who desire to have a nightmare will find a harness in the refrigerator.

9.—Each room will be furnished with a coal scuttle in the summer time, and an ice cream freezer in winter.

10.—When a bride and groom appear at breakfast for the first time nobody will refer to them as table spoons or remark that they look weary.

11.—Any guest who thinks his bill exhorbitant may argue the question with the bull terrier who is kept in the back yard for that purpose.

12.—If your room is too warm open the window and see the fire escape.

13 —In case of fire, jump out of the window and turn to the left.

14.—Those who register as man and wife, beware, for remember, God sees all.

15.—If the bell boy doesn't come when you call just run down to the office and report the matter.

16.—When there is no light in your room, open a pillow and take out a feather, which is light enough for any one.

17.—Breakfast from 7 to 8, dinner from hand to mouth, and supper if there is anything left. Guests will leave the table because it is hard wood and not digestible.

18.—Don't kick about the towel in the wash room; hundreds have wiped on it, and said nothing.

19.—Don't pack off the hardwood toothpicks for kindling; the porter will build a fire in your room for a quarter.

20.—The mammoth stove in the lobby burns nothing but wax candles, one at a time. It will be painted red next month.

The smile on the landlord's face is natural, but don't mean anything. That V on his forehead is also natural, and means that his time is worth $5 a minute.

21.—Meat drummers will deposit their valuables in the safe and pay board in advance.

*Charles Stilwell lays down the law for the Strater - Durango Democrat, Sept. 27, 1901*

# MAYO

## The Great Healing Power

As he appeared before the Royalties of Europe. Founder of the Famous Mayo Remedies.

Rheumatic Cripples made to walk. Tape Worms removed. Asthma and Catarrh cured within a few minutes by the most wonderful treatment of the age. Nothing like it ever before seen or heard of. Thousands always attend the healing and lectures.

## Mayo, the Wonder Worker of London, will be at the Strater Hotel, Wednesday, July 30.

The Lame, the Blind, the Deaf, the Rheumatic, the Paralytic and the Asthmatic will be cured without cost and without price (provided that the Rheumatic and Paralytic are on crutches or canes) by a new system of medicine imported from Europe. No magnetic healing; no laying on of hands or faith cure.

Mayo, the great English Healer and Lecturer, who has created such a sensation in all parts of America by his extraordinary cures, will cure a number of Rheumatic and Paralytic Cripples (persons on canes and on crutches), Asthma and Catarrh Sufferers.

Private Lecture to Ladies Only, Friday Night, August 1st. Subject: "Maid, Wife and Mother."

Startling Lecture to Men Only, Saturday, August 2d, at 8 p. m.

OFFICE STRATER HOTEL, HOURS 10 A. M. TO 4 P. M.

*The Durango Democrat, July 31, 1902*

## GOOD SHOW COMING.

Manager Stilwell has secured, through an open date, what will probably be one of the best and largest shows to appear in Durango this season, when Eller's big company of thirty people traveling in their own (2) special cars, will present Joseph Jefferson's version of the famous play "Rip Van Winkle," at the opera house Wednesday, July 26, staged with a complete outfit of special scenery. A first class production is guaranteed, six clever secialties being introduced, and excellent music furnished by Eller's concert band and operatic orchestra. A free band concert and unicycle exhibition will be given at noon. Doors open at 7:15, performance at 8:30.

Prices 50 and 25 cents  Tickets in advance at Parsons' drug store.

*Durango Democrat,  May 23, 1905*

## Entertained at the Strater.

It was a May party and one of those social functions that are long remembered, for a charming hostess is always to be remembered.

Miss Irene E. Baker, assisted by Miss Stilwell, entertained at the Strater last evening thirty guests assembled and the time was spent pleasantly with cards and the golden moments flitted by while the strains of sweet music was rendered.

Lunch was served in the spacious dining room and it was thoroughly enjoyed. Midst beautiful May baskets of pink, tied with white ribbon on which was the inscription "May Day, 1902," the exquisite lunch was partaken of. The ladies were each presented with carnations and the gentlemen with buttonhole bouquets. It was with happiness that the guests departed, as they had been entertained in a most charming and befitting manner.

*Durango Democrat,  May 02, 1902*

So far this season there have been more tourists and capitalists visiting this section of Colorado than ever before. Manager Stilwell of the Strater is just now at his wit's end to accommodate these parties. Today he is trying to arrange for a party of twenty-four, in charge of Major Cooper, who have been inspecting San Juan county properties.

*Durango Democrat, July 26, 1904*

# The Strater Hotel 1895 - 1926

*Henry Strater's brother, Fred, continued to live in Durango up until 1909. He was the last of the Straters to leave Durango. He was 60 years old when he moved to Denver, the city nicknamed the "Queen of the Plains". The news clips below range from humorous to heartfelt including Fred's daughter Gertrude's wedding in 1906 and his farewell dinner at the Strater hotel in December of 1908.*

### THE WEDDING

Of Miss Gertrude Strater and H. Wayne Russell as announced in the Democrat yesterday morning occurred at high noon at the beautiful boulevard home of the Strater's. Some 60 guests were present and enjoyed with the happy couple the occasion. No detail was overlooked. What was most impressive was the absolute simplicity in demeanor of everyone interested. And happy, big hearted Fred Strater was a young as his beautiful daughter. He said: "Take her, Wayne: she is all I have, and when I give her to you I give everything," and the young man felt that his newly made father-in-law spoke the truth.

The happy couple left on the delayed train for Silverton, with no clouds in the sky. May there never be any in the sky of the wedded life is the prayer of The Democrat.

*Durango Democrat, October 25, 1906*

### BABY BOY

Born to Mr. and Mrs. Wayne Russell of Denver, a baby boy. All nicely and Grandpa Fred Strater will about engage in a plug hat. Good boy.

*Durango Democrat, September 14, 1907*

Fred Strater and ten pounds extra, are back from the annual visit to that grand son at Denver. Fred will balk at a Chinese restaurant for the next two weeks.

*Durango Democrat, September 1, 1908*

### BANQUET TO MR. STRATER

On Thursday evening a farewell dinner was given to Fred Strater at the Strater Hotel by Rev. Father Callanan and the St. Columba's choir. For twenty years Mr. Strater has been connected with the Catholic church choir, and it is largely owing to his zeal and talent that the choir has reached such an eminence in musical circles. At the close of the banquet Father Callanan presented Mr. Strater with an elegant smoking set expressing the wish that in his leisure moments Mr. Strater would often recall his old tried and true friends of Durango.

Mr. Strater in a few well chosen words assured all that whatever pleasures and friendships the Queen City of the Plains would have in store for him, that Durango and its citizens in general and St. Columba's choir in particular, would always hold the first place in his affections. After an enjoyable evening, the members of the party individually tendered to Mr. Strater their best wishes for his success and happiness in his new home.

*Durango Democrat, December 19, 1908*

Fred Strater left for Denver Tuesday morning where he will make his future home. Everybody likes Fred and his family and all regret their going away. Here's hoping that they prosper and be healthy and happy wherever their lots may be cast.

*Durango Wage Earner, December 24, 1908*

98

The Gallotti Investment company is about to move its offices to the room in the Strater hotel building formerly occupied as a theater. The room is being overhauled and partitioned off and these good people assure us that they will be housed in the finest offices in Durango and prepared to open a campaign for the handling of real estate, insurance, loans and everything else that pertains to their line. They are an awful good class of people to tie to as is evidenced by their wonderful increase of business the past summer. John Turner and Joe Woods are rustlers and deserve to succeed.

*Durango Democrat, December 09, 1909*

Fred Balcom was trying to sing the baby to sleep the other evening at the Strater Hotel and a heartless wretch in the adjoining room called to him and requested that the child be permitted to cry itself to sleep.

*Durango Democrat, May 18, 1909*

## The Gallotti Investment Comp'y.

**Have Removed Their Offices to the STRATER HOTEL BLOCK**

They have all kinds of Real Estate and Insurance.

**RENTALS A SPECIALTY**

*Durango Democrat, December 31, 1909*

## STRATER HOTEL

### Leading Hotel of Durango

All rooms steam heated and cleaned by Vacuum

*Durango Democrat, December 30, 1909*

# The Strater Hotel  1895 - 1926

*The Strater Opera House was in operation in the 1890's and on in to the early 1900's. Prior to their moving out of Durango, Henry Strater's wife Carrie, entertained the guests here playing the piano. The Opera House had a reputation of acquiring some of the best entertainment available for the times.*

*Columbian & Strater Hotels in 1895 with the Opera House*

The "Flower Queen" will hold a reception at the Strater opera house on next Tuesday and Wednesday evenings. All are invited to call on her. Court dress not required.

*Advertisement for the Strater Opera House in the
Durango Wage Earner, Aug. 25, 1898*

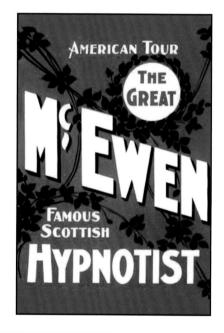

"Uncle Josh Perkins," a rural play that appears at the Strater Opera House on Nov. 27, possesses much that cannot often be said in referring to productions bearing similar titles, its motive and plot being entirely different. In "Uncle Josh Perkins," the author has reversed the usual order of things and has furnished a story that does not hinge on a mortgage or a stolen deed. The play opens in New York City and closes on "Uncle Josh's" farm, up in Vermont, in which the characters, it is said, get as close to nature as possible, making it unusually lifelike and realistic to the auditor. The company, it is declared, is way above the average and the specialties as strong as are presented in the best vaudeville houses in the country.

*Advertisement for the Strater Opera House in
the Durango Democrat, Nov. 22, 1906*

The Great McEwen

Will give a Special Performance
:: at the ::

Strater Opera House

**3 Nights** COMMENCING THURSDAY SEPT. 30 SATURDAY OCT. 2

:: Ladies Class ::

*Philip Hartley McEwen, a Famous Scottish Magician and
Hypnotist performed at the Strater while on his American
tour in 1909 - Durango Democrat, Oct 2, 1909*

# The Strater Hotel 1895 - 1926

*Very little had been known about Hattie Mashburn, the co-partner with Charles Stillwell of Stilwell & Co. who leased the Strater Hotel over 100 years ago. Discovery of the following articles shed new light on her life. We now know that she came from North Carolina, had some health issues and died in 1910.*

Miss Hattie Mashburn returned Saturday evening from her trip east. She spent two weeks at the world's fair and then went on for a visit at her old home, Old Fort, North Carolina. That is near Ashville, the place that was given such a boom on account of the Vanderbilts locating there.

*Durango Wage Earner Nov. 24, 1904*

Miss Hattie Mashburn is growing a new foot. It will have one toe and no heel. Those corns, those bunions, those trouble.

*Evidently Hattie Mashburn was having some health issues. For those who wanted privacy, evidently the early 1900's was not a good time to live in.*
*Durango Democrat, Sep. 24, 1904*

Miss Hattie Mashburn, for many years one of the lessees of the Strater hotel at Durango, died last week.

*Bayfield Blade, May 05, 1910*

The Strater cement walks being placed by Pete McLelland are the best, or among the best, in the city. It adds materially to looks of the hotel. Good work lasts, bum work is an expense account.

*The Strater is among the first to get cement sidewalks in Durango.*
*Durango Democrat, July 4, 1909*

Tom Graden started into the Strater dining room yesterday morning barefooted, but Manager Stilwell found a pair of cabbage sacks for socks and borrowed Sam May's slippers. Tom always likes to get right next to nature.

*Going into the Strater Dining room barefooted made front page news!*
*Durango Democrat, July 1, 1909*

# The Strater Hotel 1895 - 1926

## CHANGE MADE AT BURNS NATL. BANK IN DURANGO

According to the Durango Democrat J. C. Campbell has resigned as president and director of the Burns National Bank of that city. He is succeeded as president by Charles E. Stillwell as president and as director by J. R. C. Tyler. The change became effective Jan. 1.

*Charles Stilwell becomes President of Burns Bank. Durango Colo.*
*Telluride Daily Journal, Jan 3, 1923*

*One of Charlie Stilwell's automobiles. The girl seated in the passenger seat might be his daughter Ada.*

# THREATS ARE SENT DURANGO BANKER

Durango, Colo., April 13.—A cordon of heavily armed policemen and sheriff's deputies was thrown around the home of Charles E. Stilwell, president of the Burns National bank of Durango late Wednesday after he received an extortion note ordering him to pay $2,500 or his home would be blown up with dynamite.

The message directed that the money be placed in a culvert five and a half miles south of Durango before 6 p. m. Wednesday.

E. D. McElroy and Howard Shields rolled in Sunday from their recent trip to Denver. They went up two weeks ago in two Studebaker cars belonging to McElroy and Chas. Stilwell of Durango. They were accompanied by Mr. Stilwell, Mrs. Stilwell and her mother and a salesman whom they picked up in Bayfield. In Denver they sold the two Studebaker cars and bought a new Commonwealth touring car which they drove home.

*Charles Stilwell loved his automobiles. This news clip was printed in the Weekly Ignacio Chieftain, August 8, 1919*

*At the turn of the Century, banks could print their own currency. This ten dollar bill printed by the Burns National Bank of Durango was signed by Charles E. Stilwell. Earl Barker Sr. was also the President of the Burns Bank some years later and printed and signed currency as well.*

# The Strater Hotel 1895 - 1926

*The newspaper article below entitled: "Titanic" Moves Fast Following a Rumpus" has particular relevance because of the location of the event. The Jarvis Livery/Garage was owned and operated by Jim Jarvis, Rod Barker's Great Grandfather. Titanic was a porter employed at the Strater Hotel in 1922.*

*Located on 2nd Avenue, The Jarvis Garage was a Studebaker Wagon Dealership. Studebaker wagons first began to be sold in 1852 for farmers, miners and the military. The first gasoline car to be fully manufactured by Studebaker was in August of 1912.*

*Jim Jarvis and his wife, Ada Ferguson, moved to Durango in 1906. In 1914, Jim Jarvis sold the first Studebaker Automobile in Colorado.*

*He also founded The Durango Film Production Company in 1917. Jarvis produced a number of movie shorts including: Small Town Vamp, Mesa Verde and Snow Wonderland. His first full length movie was Love of a Navajo. Released in 1922 and premiering at the Gem Theater in Durango, this movie received nationwide distribution.*

*Jim led a colorful and active life. Of particular interest is that he was a close friend of Richard Weatherill, who is famous for re-discovering the Mesa Verde Cliff Dwellings in 1888. Jim would frequently explore the cliff dwellings with Richard.*

*Jim Jarvis's son Irvin, was Jentra Barker's father. Jentra is the mother of Rod Barker, the current owner (in 2009) of the Strater Hotel, making Jim Jarvis, Rod Barker's Great Grandfather.*

## "TITANIC" MOVES FAST FOLLOWING A RUMPUS

The Jarvis garage was the scene of wild excitement shortly after the noon hour. today when W. P. Hensley of Largo Canon, N. M., took two shots at "Titanic," the negro employed as porter at the Strater hotel. No damage was done and after the melee was over the last seen of the porter was when he was headed in rapid flight up Second avenue. toward the court house.

There is a variance of stories as to what led up to the shooting. It is alleged that the porter and a white man had been drinking "bootleg" liquor out of the same bottle which action, it is alleged, was objected to by Hensley. Hensley and "Titanic" met each other outside of the Jarvis garage. There was a rush and the two were on the ground. It is alleged that Hensley drew his pistol and shot twice at the porter who was holding his arms. The shots went wild but almost struck Jim Jarvis and Dr. Haggart who were

*Titanic, the Strater Porter has a run in with an angry man and takes off running up Second Avenue.*
*(Unfortunately, the rest of the article is not available.)*
*Telluride Daily Journal, Sep 16, 1922*

Purchased Two Studebakers – Mayor C. F. Loebnitz of Telluride yesterday bought a Studebaker "six" from J. W. Jarvis, the local agent and W. M. Anderson purchased a Studebaker "Four." Both cars were bought on 30 days Delivery.- Durango Democrat

*Jim Jarvis sells the first Studebaker Auto in Colorado.*
*Telluride Daily Journal, Mar. 11, 1914*

-J. W. Jarvis, the Durango automobile dealer, came up from his headquarters Saturday night to see that the shipment of Studebaker cars for Messrs. Loebnitz and Anderson landed here safely. He will remain in the city a short time and may inoculate other local residents with automobile virus.

*The paper forewarns residents of Mr. Jarvis being in town and possibly "inoculating " residents with the "automobile virus."*
*Telluride Daily Journal, Apr. 27, 1914*

# The Strater Hotel 1895 - 1926

Announcement of new Strater management
Silverton Standard, December 25, 1920

## STRATER HOTEL BUILDING SOLD TO COLORADO MEN

Late this afternoon the confirmation of the sale of the Strater hotel building by Thos. MacBeth of Cleveland, O., to Messrs. Hamilton of Pueblo and Heeley of Walsenburg was given out by John Turner of the Turner Investment Co., which had been agents for the building and who engineered the sale. The consideration was not given out but it is rumored to have been in the neghborhood of $45,000.—Durango Herald.

*Telluride Daily Journal, Monday July 10, 1922*

## ONE SHINE WINS BIG AUTO FOR HOTEL PORTER

How would you like to buy a ticket in a contest for an eighteen hundred dollar automobile, trade the ticket for a shine and then find that your number had won the car? This is just about what happened to Otto Fischer, assistant manager of the Strater hotel, for a ticket he purchased in an American Legion contest at Alamosa more than a year ago and sold to "Big Bill" Jackson, porter at an Alamosa hotel, for a shine and sixty cents was returned a winner in the final count last Saturday night. The automobile is a 7-passenger, six-cylinder Studebaker car, and the funniest thing about it all, is that Fischer hasn't yet received the 60 cents. All he got was the shine.—Durango Democrat.

*Strater Porter wins Luxury Auto*
*Telluride Daily Journal, March 10, 1923*

## STARTER HOTEL BUILDING WAS SOLD ON TUESDAY

The Strater hotel building in Durango was sold Tuesday, says the Durango Democrat, the consideration being $40,000. The owners, Thomas and Andrew MacBeth of Cleveland sold to E. L. Neeley of Walsenburg and H. H. Hamilton of Pueblo. What the new owners will do with their new acquisition has not been announced.

*Another announcement of the sale of the Strater Hotel in 1922*
*Telluride Daily Journal, Friday August 4, 1922*

## BUILD ADDITION TO THE STRATER HOTEL

An addition to the annex of the Strater hotel, says the Durango Democrat, has been started. Seven additional rooms will be built, in order to accomodate the rapidly increasing business of this popular hostelry.

*Following the annex of the Columbian Hotel into the Strater in 1902, this is the first addition to be added to the hotel. Telluride Daily Journal Feb 1, 1923*

# Chapter Five
# 5

# 1926—2009
# The Barker's Take the Reins

Earl Barker Jr.
and Dancer in 1991

# 1926—2009 The Barker's Take the Reins

*The decade leading up* to 1926 was by no means a prosperous time for the nation. World War I had ended on November 11, 1918. The war claimed an estimated 16 million lives. In 1918, the influenza epidemic swept the world killing an estimated 50 million people. One fifth of the world's population was attacked by this deadly virus. Within months, it had killed more people than any other illness in recorded history. Durango and the surrounding area were not spared from these tragedies. According to the Center of Southwest Studies, (Fort Lewis College) 1 out of every 15 people in the area died because of this epidemic.

The Strater Hotel was not prospering during this time. It had changed hands a number of times within recent years, and was in need of an owner that would bring the Strater back to the stature that it had enjoyed during its younger years. In 1926 the hotel business was not thriving as it is today. Travel was still limited, due to the quality of the roads, and automobiles were still a rather new invention; not a possession of the majority. The hotel was nearly forty years old and was in need of major updating. Keep in mind that at the time of construction, there were only seven bathrooms, it was built with no electricity, no plumbing and no central heating. Some utilities had been upgraded over the past forty years, but much more was needed.

In 1926, a group of Five local businessmen formed a corporation named *The New Strater Corporation*. These men included Charles F. Van Brimmer, Earl Barker, C. E. Moore, John W. Turner, and A. W. Robbins. They purchased the hotel for $40,000. Mr. C. F. Van Brimmer managed the hotel from 1926 to 1929. In 1929, J. A. Segerberg was hired on as the active manager. During the 1930's Earl Barker and J. A. Segerberg purchased the shares of the other

*Compare this photo (above) taken between 1935-7, prior to the 1938 addition, to the photo on the following page taken in the 1950's that shows the addition.*

*Courtesy of Roderick E. Barker*

# 1926—2009 The Barker's Take the Reins

four original stockholders until both Earl Barker and J. A. Segerberg each owned 50% interest in the hotel. Later, Barker and Segerberg decided to bring in a third shareholder to intervene in case of a stalemate on an important decision regarding the hotel. That final shareholder of just 1% was Alice Bane. For the first number of years, the partnership worked well. The new owners of the hotel reinvested time and money into the stately Strater. First, they gave special attention to modernizing the rooms. This included a $3,000 expenditure for all new furniture.

Up until 1933, Earl Barker and his associates also had to deal with the Prohibition years. This had started in 1920 and ran for 13 years. However, a certain Johnny McNamara, who eventually ended up owning Nickles Electric, worked as a bellhop at the Strater during his younger years. During the Prohibition era, he hid bootleg liquor under the Strater elevator! He made a lot of money with this small franchise and probably made a lot of guests very happy as well!

As business increased during the 1930's, Earl Barker and Segerberg saw the need for additional rooms. In 1938, a large addition was started to be built on the west side of the original building, nicknamed the "Back Forty." The 40 room addition and renovation was completed in February, 1941. These new rooms offered comfort and style comparable to accommodations found in larger cities including twin Beds, tiled bathrooms and comfortable furniture.

Just after completion, on February 24th, 1941, the National Guard of Durango were called to active duty. With a burst of patriotism, Mr. Segerberg, the manager of the hotel since 1929, invited the National Guard Unit-168th Field Artillery to be the first guests in the new addition.

*The Strater in the 1950's.*

# 1926—2009 The Barker's Take the Reins

The soldiers, 73 men strong, were free guests of the hotel for ten days before shipping out. The rooms were then opened to the public.

The clientele was changing for the Strater. For many years, the salesmen who came to town selling their wares and "setting up shop" at the hotel had been a component that the Strater could count on. As time went on, with the onset of larger department stores, mass production of most products and the popularity of automobiles making travel so much easier, the traveling salesmen coming to town with their trunks was no longer a viable reality. Management recognized the need to draw a new type of guest to the Strater. They recognized the fact that they had to be able to attract tourists. In order to do so, additional changes had to be made.

The Strater had seen great improvements in certain areas. The furniture in the rooms had been updated. New, more modern rooms had been added on. Still, there was much that had to be updated. The basic components that made up the basic functioning of the structure including the plumbing system, the electrical wiring, bathrooms and much more needed attention.

Earl Barker Sr. was keenly aware of these needs and wanted to move on these issues. Unfortunately, his partner of many years had receded from his earlier motivation of wanting to stick money into the Strater. He was up in the years now, and no longer had the motivation that he had when younger. When it came to voting, the neutral partner, Alice Bane ended up not being truly neutral. She always favored her friend Segerberg. This inability to move forward proved to be very frustrating to Earl Barker Sr.

*Earl Barker Sr. in 1954*

He knew that if this couldn't be resolved and soon, that his years of investment including time and money into the Strater could end up in total collapse. He decided to act.

In 1954 Earl Barker Sr. purchased the entire stock of the hotel. The Strater Hotel became a single family operation for the first time in its history. He would own, manage and operate the hotel with the assistance of his son, Earl Jr. and later, be joined by his son-in-law Robert Blomstrom.

In order to attract tourists, entertainment was one of the first items on the list that they focused on. The corner office that once housed the original Strater Bar, then Turner Investments, and finally the State of Colorado Employment Agency, was looked at closely. Earl Jr. and Bob Blomstrom saw the need for an upstanding bar. Earl Sr. on the other hand, frowned on the idea stating, *"We'll never make more profit in a bar than the $25 per month that we're making from the office rental."* His son and son-in law knew that there was no way they would get his permission. By the same token, Earl Jr. inherited the grit of his father. He had total faith that his idea was the way to go and he wasn't going to give up. The Diamond Belle Saloon is here today because of his hardheadedness.

# 1926—2009 The Barker's Take the Reins

*The Diamond Belle Saloon at the Strater Hotel with the famous pianist,*
*Al Rose of the Al Rose Trio. Al would perform regularly at the Strater.*

He figured out a plan. Earl Sr. loved to get away from the cold and snow during the winter months. He left for Hawaii, one of his favorite destinations. Earl Jr. and his brother-in-law Bob, along with their wives Jentra and Marge, figured that it was easier to gain forgiveness than to get permission. After his father's departure to Hawaii, Earl Jr. went to work incorporating the plans that designer Robert Klein of Albuquerque had drawn up to create the Diamond Belle Saloon. The work went along beautifully and on time. By the time his father returned from his stay in Hawaii, the Saloon had been completed. The final piece of the puzzle was put into place. When Earl Sr. entered the hotel, he walked into the new Saloon and saw it filled with all of his best friends, enjoying themselves! He realized that the idea to put in a new bar was his idea all along! In this way, the Strater's journey into Victorian charm began.

The Strater had already been standing for 67 years when the Barker family became the sole owners. Earl Sr. along with his son and son-in-law, had the wisdom to see that you needed a sound efficient structure as a base to build on. The Diamond Belle Saloon was just the beginning. The "T. L. C." that the Strater was about to receive would be second to none!

# 1926—2009 The Barker's Take the Reins

Earl Jr. and Bob Blomstrom's intention was to give the hotel a major overhaul. So the transformation of the old "Strater House" began from the basement level, on up to the rooftop. The utilities were the first to receive attention including; the air conditioning and heating; new wiring and plumbing. They then went to work upgrading all the bathrooms and also installing in-room closets. No area escaped upgrading. As you can only imagine, projects of this nature are huge on an individual scale, for a single family home. It is almost beyond comprehension to visualize the magnitude of these projects on a structure, the size of the Strater! Despite this, Earl Barker Sr. along with this son and son-in-law, moved forward and successfully accomplished their goals and improvements.

The timing of these changes to the Strater couldn't have happened at a better time. It was while traveling back to Durango from a race at Crested Butte, that Ray Duncan, an avid skier and supporter of junior ski racing commented to his colleague Chet Andersen: *"it's a pity that young Durango skiers don't have a big mountain where they could ski and train."*[56] Andersen said he knew of such a big mountain 25 miles north of Durango. He took Duncan to the spot. That's all it took. Duncan formed a development company, Forest Service permits were acquired, money was raised, and land was purchased from local owners for the base area. Purgatory opened for skiers in 1965. This began a whirlwind of ski resort development. Purgatory is best known for having some of the most consistent snow anywhere. The virtual guarantee of snow combined with the best ski weather in America added to the huge success of this ski resort. Within short order, arrangements were made for bus tours of skiers to stop over at Durango. The Strater played a major role in this since the skiers would naturally stay at the Hotel! The additional patrons proved to be very good for the Strater. In earlier years, you'll recall that the winter months were so lean that there was talk of draining the water pipes, shutting off the furnace and closing the hotel down for the season. Having the skiers as an ongoing customer base in the winter was a major plus.

Another development added to the success of the Strater. During the 1960's, Tauck Tours, one of the largest tour companies in the world, started coming to Durango. They would stop their bus right in front of the Strater and unload bus load after busload five times each week! The visitors would stay over for two nights. The guests would tour Mesa Verde on the first day and take the railroad to Silverton on the second.

Rumblings of the railroad pulling out continued to surface during these years. Thankfully, a number of people including Earl Barker Jr., realized that the railroad had potential for tourism. So, they were preparing to invest in the railroad. The New Strater Corporation purchased 20 shares of the Durango-Silverton Railroad Company. The stock certificate was #04. In 1981, Charles E. Bradshaw stepped up and purchased the entire stock of the D&RGW railroad and renamed it the Durango & Silverton Narrow Gauge Railroad. Durango now had a railroad which would begin gearing up for tourism rather than just typical commercial use.

Without a doubt, the Strater's future was shining bright!

*Earl Barker Sr. standing at the Strater Hotel entrance, Circa 1960*

*Based upon the calendar hanging on the wall, this photo has a date stamp of April 4, 1955. This is the Strater Lobby Desk with Bob Blomstrom to the left (bow tie) and Earl Barker Jr. (center) assisting a guest.*

*Photo of the Lobby in the late 1960's.*

# REWARD

# $000,000,000.50

**Robert L. Blomstrom:** Alias - Doc, Bookie, Whittles.

**Wanted for:** Impersonating a cocktail waitress, Pinching cuties, and making Hooch.

**Caution!** This dastardly rapscallion has been know to charm women and children. He is also guilty of several marketing schemes know to have improved this Hotel. If seen, lay off the scotch!

# REWARD

# $000,000,000.50

**Earl A. Barker:** Alias - Bunko, Baby Face, Junior, Hobbles & Earlie D'Bark.

**Wanted for:** Impersonating a Bartender, Pinching pennies, and making Mayhem.

**Caution!** This is a devious and dastardly character who will stop at nothing to have a good time. Has been seen signing bar tabs as the owner. Use caution!

# 1926—2009 The Barker's Take the Reins

*The Strater Coffee Shop in the middle 1950's (Location of the present day Mahogany Grille)*

# 1926—2009 The Barker's Take the Reins

Of all the rooms in the Strater, perhaps no area has undergone more change over the last century than the room that hosts one of Durango's current premier restaurants, the Mahogany Grille. Originally built in 1893 as part of the Columbian Hotel, note the following:

In 1893, this room was the Durango Opera House. This was a center for Durango entertainment.

In the early 1900's, the Durango Opera House was replaced by the restaurant named the Red Lantern Inn.

By the 1930's, the restaurant was renovated and renamed the "Strater Coffee Shop".

After some 30 years, another renovation occurred in the early 1960's, resulting in the opening of the popular "Terrace Restaurant". **

The friendly employees that made "The Terrace" a great success in Durango.

The Terrace was replaced by the Opera House in the 1970's.

Henry's Chop house followed the Opera house. On Mar 17, 2004, The Mahogany Grille opened its doors to the public. Having enjoyed many of the entrée's offered here, I give the Mahogany Grille a 10 for excellence in quality, taste, uniqueness, presentation and ambience. My all time favorite dish is their Pepper Steak Herbert!

*** In The 1960's Earl and Jentra Barker were conferring with Bob Klein, a consulting designer regarding the naming of the new restaurant. The Barkers were leaning toward naming the new restaurant "The Gazebo". Bob voiced his feelings and stated that he didn't feel that "The Gazebo" would be a fitting name. When asked why, he went and picked up a dictionary and turned to the "G"s and found **Gazebo: (Definition) - an erection in the garden**. At that point, the decision was unanimous and the name was changed to "The Terrace".*

# 1926—2009 The Barker's Take the Reins

*The Strater in the 1950's*

*Located downstairs, this lounge was named the "Snake Pit" in the 1950's.*
*Today, this room is home to the beautiful Centennial Room. (see Page 143)*

# 1926—2009 The Barker's Take the Reins

*The Strater as it looked in the 1950's*

# 1926—2009 The Barker's Take the Reins

Earl Barker Jr.—Manager of the
Strater Hotel & Coffee Shop in 1956

In the photo below, Earl Barker Jr. is proudly displaying his new 6 foot tall RadaRange.[R] At the time of the photo, 1959, this was new "state of the art" technology. The technology to cook food using microwaves had been discovered accidently in 1945. The person who discovered this ability was Percy Spencer. He was working for a company named Raytheon. This company manufactured Magnetrons. Magnetrons are used to generate the microwave radio signals that are the core mechanism of Radar. In 1945 Percy Spencer was standing in front of an operating magnetron, when he realized that the peanut chocolate bar in his pocket was heating up and melting! He realized that the radar had melted his candy with microwaves!

The first food to be deliberately cooked with microwaves was popcorn. Eggs were attempted next, but they exploded right in the face of the person doing the test! A number of years went by. The technology was applied to the cooking of food. Like anything new, it was very expensive. The first commercial microwave was introduced to the world in 1954. This was an early model that consumed 1600 watts and carried a price tag of nearly $3000! The average annual income in 1954 was $3,900 and the average home cost $22,000. The cost of $3000 for an oven was a large sum of money!

Earl Barker Jr., the smart businessman that he was, recognized the value of this new invention and had the insight to see that the benefits far outweighed the cost. Thus, the Strater was among the first in the nation to acquire this technology.

The first microwave ovens stood nearly 6 foot tall and weighed nearly 750 lbs.

119

# 1926—2009 The Barker's Take the Reins

*There have been ongoing changes and improvements in the Strater over the course of its 120 plus year history. An example of this is the area known today as "The Office Spiritorium." Originally, in 1881, this room housed the Strater Bros. Paints & Oils Store. In 1888 it became the first barbershop in Durango. It was converted into the lobby of the Columbian Hotel in 1893. In the early 1900's this room became the Strater Barbershop again. In the 1960's Earl Barker Jr. transformed the barbershop into a private club for area oil and gas executives, naming it the Durango Petroleum Club. In the late 1970's, this popular meeting space was renovated and became a banquet room named the Columbian Room. In 2000, "The Office" opened its doors as a smoke free Victorian Spiritorium. The Office Spiritorium is furnished with lush furniture, antique typewriters and unique memorabilia. A lavish hand-carved fireplace compliments its cozy atmosphere. Current photos of the Office are located in chapter 6 entitled: "Photo Tour of the Strater".*

*Photos below:*
1. *The Petroleum Club during a banquet in 1968.*
2. *Bar area for the Petroleum Room*
3. *Seating and décor of the Petroleum Club*

# 1926—2009 The Barker's Take the Reins

## Henry Strater Theater

In 1961, the bold plan of converting the Dodge Automobile Garage building next door to the Strater, into a theatre was undertaken. The idea of creating an attraction that would appeal to Durango visitors was fairly new to Durango, but fundamental in the minds of Earl and Jentra Barker, and greatly supported by Jentra's mother, Marion Jarvis. The garage repair shop was a sore detraction to the downtown area. It fought with the image that the Strater was trying to develop for the Central Business District. The garage was leased from the Anesi family. Plans were drawn up and the area was remodeled into a shopping arcade and a quaint little theatre that would hold about 225 people. The theme of the plays was to be aimed at the "Turn-of-the-Century", to give guests of the hotel, and the community an appreciation for the old times, and to poke fun at the stuffy morals of the Victorian era. The Theatre's Victorian design was the work of Robert Klein, who also did the Diamond Belle Saloon in previous years. It was determined that Melodrama's would be a great vehicle to deliver fun and the feeling of yester years to the entire family.

Searches for a competent director lead them to Orvis Grout from Colorado Springs. With a lot of hard work, and plenty of financial risk, the Theatre opened to a packed house on June 23, 1962. Times weren't always easy though, as Durango tourism trade was in its infancy. To spread the risk, the Diamond Circle Theatre Company was formed as a partnership with Earl and Jentra Barker, Marion Jarvis, Orvis Grout, Mort McGinley, Robert Beers and Mahlon White. Over the years the gamble paid off. Today, it is estimated that the theatre performed to a total audience of over 600,000 people during the summers of 1962 thru 2007. Two period plays were presented on alternative nights for each summer season.

From the late 1980's, Earl and Jentra's daughter, Jeannie Barker Wheeldon, participated in the theatre in all levels, from actress to director and theatre manager and finally owner of the Diamond Circle Melodrama Company. At a very young age, she intently memorized the lines of each actor during the spring rehearsals and later trained under Director Orvis Grout to learn his unique style of direction.

In 2007, with new interests calling, Jeannie decided to retire and sold the Diamond Circle Melodrama name and production company to a neighboring community theatre, called The Durango Arts Center, where it ran for the 2008 summer season. The hotel's theatre was rebranded the Henry Strater Theatre, and produced 2 musicals for the summer season followed by a variety of outstanding talent from all over the continent. This theatre (still under lease from the Anesi family) operates year-round as a community meeting space, hosting festivals and events for the entire community. It remains one of the oldest continuously running theatres in Colorado..

2010 will mark the return of melodrama to the Henry Strater Theatre.

# 1926—2009 The Barker's Take the Reins

*Entrance into the Henry Strater Theater*

*The Diamond Circle Theatre (later renamed the Henry Strater Theatre)
with cast members rehearsing.*

# 1926—2009 The Barker's Take the Reins

*Earl & Jentra Barker*

In 1963, Earl and Jentra traveled to a hotel convention in Atlanta, GA. Earl spent his time attending the meetings and Jentra enjoyed the shopping. Jentra found a great little antique store with a spectacular Victorian[1] bed. She theorized that a vintage hotel might be fun to furnish with vintage furniture. Talking it over with Earl, they decided to give it a try and purchased enough American Victorian walnut furniture to furnish five rooms. The two of them cashed in their airplane tickets and drove back from the convention in a U-Haul truck, stopping at several antique stores along the way. The original bed that Jentra found is located in room 322 and is shown below. This began the hotel's collection of American Victorian-era walnut furniture.[2] Today, the Strater has attained museum status, having the largest collection of American Victorian walnut furniture in the world!

The Victorian-era bed pictured here was in poor condition when it was first found. Spanish Moss that had been used to stuff the upholstery was ratty looking and falling out. The Barkers had the bed repaired and cleaned up. As you can see from the photo, it is truly a beautiful piece of furniture.

The five furnished rooms with Victorian-era furniture ended up being the most popular rooms in the hotel. They were filled all of the time. Because of this, Earl and Jentra began a mission to find this unique beautiful American Victorian-era furniture. Earl, having been a pilot in the air force, owned a plane and decided to use this as a means of traveling to various towns and destinations throughout the country. He would fly out with his wife Jentra, and also another pilot. Stopping at various locations, they would visit the local antique stores, find pieces of furniture that they liked, and then prepay for it. They then shuttled back to the plane and went to their next destination, repeating the activity. Once they had enough to fill up a truck, the pilot that had been with them, would fly the plane back. Earl and Jentra would rent a truck, pick up the furniture at the various locations and drive back to Durango. This became a passion that began the transformation of the Strater Hotel into the distinctive Victorian Luxury hotel it is today.

[1] Victorian furnishings relate to Queen Victoria of Britain and Ireland who reigned from 1837 to 1901. Her choice of furnishings was a highly ornamented, massive style of architecture. Queen Victoria's love for this type of furniture was so overwhelming, that when she would travel, her subjects were expected to refurnish their homes in this style of furniture. If they didn't, they would not be honored with her visit again. The approval of the Queen was of supreme importance, so the majority followed in suite. In time this type of furniture was named Victorian.
[2] American Victorian walnut is distinctive in that it is made of solid walnut. Because of the scarcity of walnut in Europe, European Victorian walnut is veneer over pine. Hence the distinction and high value of American Victorian walnut.

# 1926—2009 The Barker's Take the Reins

In 1983, after great consideration and 23 years of hard work, Earl and Jentra decided to sell the hotel and retire. Their son Rod along with his wife Laurie were living in Kansas City. Rod was employed at the time by the Westin Crown Center Hotel and was training in hotel management.

Working for a Corporate hotel chain, Rod realized the distinction that the Strater held. It wasn't a "cookie cutter" hotel as most are, that make up the large chains. Having been raised in and around the Strater, Rod wasn't ready to part with this landmark hotel. Also, for several years, Rod and Laurie had been assisting his parents, hunting for antique furniture throughout the Midwest. Having completed his management training, he felt that he was ready to continue the Barker family legacy by assuming the management role of the Strater.

*Roderick E. Barker*

When Rod and Laurie Barker returned from Kansas City, the Strater didn't look like the gemstone it does today. They returned to a hotel in need of a makeover. Eight years of operation, without the needed influx of cash to continue to build and restore the hotel, left it a gem without polish. The guestroom's wall decorations were semi-modern; the drapes were funky 1960's era prints and the carpets were worn out. Guest conveniences were insufficient too: the air-conditioning system was constantly failing; frequent power failures were bringing the operation to a stop; the public meeting and dining facilities were not focused on the needs of the local and visiting public and major competition was on its way. Rod's work was cut out for him. He began to do research into wall coverings used during the Victorian Era. He traveled around the country to learn about techniques and designs to start a second phase renovation. His mom

*Laurie & Rod Barker dressed in period attire during an annual Open House festivity.*

Jentra joined him at an interior design seminar in Dallas where he found resources to help the mammoth project in front of him. One of the best finds was at the Historic Molly Brown House in Denver. There Rod found out about Bradbury and Bradbury wallpapers. This was a real breakthrough because there were very few great wall coverings made that could bring the level of elegance that Rod was looking for. Unfortunately they were quite expensive, but then aren't most high quality items?

Rod began by working on the guest rooms. The cost of a single guest room was around $12,000 just to provide wallpaper, carpet and the beautiful heavy velvet draperies that grace the windows. This was at a time when the economy was sluggish and money was in short supply. However, there was to be no stopping because the very future of the hotel was at stake. Rod remembers when the CEO of a large national chain that built a competing hotel in Durango, sat down in the Diamond Belle Saloon at a table next to him to have a drink. The CEO

124

said to his friend, *"I wonder how long it will take before we put this little place out of business."* Rod remembers that question each time he feels that work is moving slowly. Because of the high cost of the renovation, Rod could only afford to renovate six to ten rooms per year. They did it right though, and the style was an immediate success with everyone but his mom and dad, who were choking over the cost. In 1989, Rod entered one of the rooms (Room 220) that he and maintenance foreman Charlie Schumacher had renovated, into the International Gold Key competition. It won one of the top three awards given in New York City at the International Hotel Show.

*Room 220*

## The Pullman Room

As time went by, more and more thought was given to the public spaces and the design that would give them flair. The opulent Pullman room was previously called the "Gold Room" and was a simple design of hardwood floors with flocked wallpaper and a sprayed on ceiling. The trim had white and gold paint. Rod and Charlie gutted the room and began adding the kind of Victorian embellishments that would stand the test of time. Mirrors were added to widen the room, beveled glass ceiling panels were placed to make the crystal chandeliers seem to float on the ceiling to give it an appearance of height that the room didn't have. The carpeting was designed to give the feeling of a Persian rug in keeping with the Victorian era. To keep with the interest of Durango's history, Rod designed the shadow boxes to line the room and framed the William Jackson railroad photographs. Since the room was long and narrow, with a coffered ceiling, it resembled a Pullman Railroad Car, so the room was named the Pullman Room. Inside the shadow boxes were placed many museum quality articles that guests could view while they enjoyed the room.

## The Lobby

Rod then turned his attention to the hotel lobby. It was a very plain looking lobby with orange carpet and a Formica covered front desk. Rod decided to completely redesign the desk and reposition it at an angle to give a welcoming feeling to guests as they entered the room. He designed the desk woodwork on his computer, as he did with the ceiling decorations. The Eastlake style woodwork was also laid out on the CADD program so that Charlie and the crew could copy the design and use the feature in all the future hotel renovations. At the back of the lobby, they added a fireplace and a half wall feature to create an area where guests could enjoy getting together with a sense of privacy. The men's restroom was redone with granite and marble accents. The grand staircase was redesigned with new woodwork to add a dramatic entrance to the rooms above. During the process, two old doorways were found, buried beneath the plaster. One went to the north into the area where the Diamond Belle Saloon was and the other went south into the old Columbian Hotel section. Rod used the north doorway to hide a large time capsule and the door to the south was opened and designed for a later entry into a future new top of the line bar. The remodel was a success and cost about $750,000 but offers hotel guests a real lobby that matched the elegance that they found in their guest rooms. To give something for the kids, there were three secret hiding places added to the lobby for secret things to be kept. The staff has fun giving clues to their locations.

## The Office Spiritorium

The next project was to design and implement a new bar in the space that was once the Columbian Hotel lobby and subsequently, the Strater barbershop and then the Durango Petroleum Club Room. The space was not fully used and had a wonderful view of Main Street that most restaurant owners would die for.

This bar was destined to be the most beautiful bar that Rod could imagine and that Charlie could build. It had to blend with the future design of a new dining room, so that the service would flow and yet the beauty would not be compromised. It took five months to design and

11 months to do the work. The room was torn down to bare walls and joists. All new infrastructure was constructed for the support of the most elegant Victorian Bar yet seen in Durango. It was named "The Office" after a Durango Bar from the 1880's with the same name. Instead of calling the room a Bar, it was called a Spiritorium since it was different from any bar around. In the namesake bar of the past, Durango's professional people would often visit after work and when they would arrive home late they

could correctly claim that they had been 'at the Office'. It seemed perfect for modern times too and working antique telephones were installed at many of the tables, so that people could call their spouses and ask them to join them at the office.

The finish work of "The Office" came from the Strater's own wood working shop. The tile work in the entry was designed after a pattern inspired from a floor in the Louvre museum in Paris and also in a 1,000+ year old ruin in Pompeii. The stones were cut in Italy. The beveled glass work was made locally by Betty Kirkpatrick and the fireplace and matching mirror was designed in the Eastlake style by Rod Barker and built by Charlie Schumacher. The front of the bar has a presentation of Two dollar bills in the face which was a fun statement to Rod's Dad because the old bar in the room was covered with One dollar bills. In the long hallway to the west and in shadowboxes around the room, there is a museum of office equipment and office artifacts, many over 120 years old.

## The Mahogany Grille

Next, the challenging design of the Mahogany Grille dining room was undertaken. This room was a daunting challenge because there were seven doorways to work with. The traffic was very disruptive to the room, so the most important part was to remove that foot-traffic while adding a classy style to the room. The Victorian Era was all about modern conveniences so Rod felt quite at home using a blend of contemporary and Victorian styles to embellish the room. The two Tiffany style glass domes are a focal point. The west dome is the original one and it was purchased from the Solid Muldoon Bar which went out of business in the 1990's. The wood embellishment was added by the hotel staff. Then the second dome was made by a previous maintenance manager, Mike Mitchell, who had just moved to Arkansas and was out of a job. Mike took about 18 months to create the replica and then drove the work to the hotel in his pickup truck. Today the two pieces are a strong statement to the room.

The mirrored buffet on the west side was purchased in Denver by Earl and Jentra Barker. It was brought from Milan Italy by Opera Star Edith Mason. Rod designed the West side of the room to accent this beautiful piece as if it was in a shadow box display. The woodwork on the entry is an Eastlake style design which adds a great deal of depth to the room, as well as a welcoming entry for guests. A rare Mason-Hamlin Symetrigrand piano compliments the Mahogany Grille as well with talented pianists entertaining the dinner guests on a nightly basis.

## The Centennial Room

Finally, the Centennial room was next to be addressed in the basement of the Columbian Hotel. This room is decorated in the Arts and Crafts Style made famous by Gustoff Stickley, architects Greene and Green and Frank Lloyd Wright. The room was made to look like it adjoined a veranda by giving the storage room etched glass doors with light from behind. The photographs in the room were taken in the 1880's by William Jackson, who also accompanied the Hayden expedition with the famous painter Thomas Moran. Jackson's photographs helped show Congress what they had acquired with the Louisiana Purchase. The rooms name was given to commemorate Marion Jarvis, Jentra Barker's mother, who was Durango's Centennial Queen. President Gerald Ford and author Louis L'Amour were both important names in the hotels guest history and were involved with Durango's 1981 Centennial Celebration.

# 1926—2009 The Barker's Take the Reins

Earl Barker Sr.　　　　　Earl Barker Jr.　　　　　Rod Barker

**Earl A. Barker Sr.** (1896-1968) Earl Sr. was originally from Geneva, Nebraska. He moved to Durango in 1924 to become President of the Burns Bank. In 1926, Earl, along with a number of other investors, purchased the Strater. He was a smart businessman who understood what it took to make an undertaking successful. Thanks to his good judgment, the Strater hasn't met the fate of a wrecking ball as have so many other hotels from this time period. By 1953, he had become the sole owner of the Strater, at which time he gave his son Earl Jr. and son-in-law Bob Blomstrom the responsibility of managing the hotel. His motto to his family was; "If we take care of the Strater, it will take care of us." He instilled this into the family and the results are obvious today.

**Earl Barker Jr.** (1928-2008) was born in Durango at Mercy Hospital on October 7, 1928. His father Earl Sr. had him start at the hotel working as a Bellhop. He married Jentra Jarvis on September 21, 1952. In 1968, Earl Jr. became the sole owner and President of the Strater Hotel. Earl was active in the Colorado Hotel and Motel Association, serving two terms as its president. He was Hotelier of the Year in 1976 and was voted into the Colorado Hotel and Motel Association Hall of Fame in 1986. He was also the chairman of the Small Property Council of the American Hotel and Motel Association. Earl retired from the day to day management of the Strater in 1979, allowing his managers to oversee the day to day affairs of the hotel. Then in 1983, his son Rod stepped in, and became actively involved in the Strater Management. Earl Jr. enjoyed a long retirement of 29 years. Even during his retirement and up until his death on September 7, 2008, he kept up his interest in the hotel, by advising and serving on the Board of Directors.

**Robert Blomstrom** (1920-2004) It is important to note that Bob Blomstrom had a role in co-managing the Strater for a time in the 1950's, along with his brother-in-law, Earl Jr. He stayed for a number of years at the Strater, but then went back to his first love, teaching. Although he left to pursue his career in teaching, his attachment to the Strater never diminished. In fact, years later, his sons Rick and Jim played an active role in the Strater as well. Rick held the position as the Food & Beverage Director of the Restaurant, while Jim was the Strater General Manager.

When Bob left the Strater, he first taught at Arizona State University in Tempe, Ariz., for five years, and then moved on to Michigan State University, in East Lansing, Mich. While at MSU, he was the director of the School of Hotel, Restaurant and Institutional Management. Bob Blomstrom retired in 1983, He and his wife Marge spent warm winters in Sun City, Arizona, and cooler summers in Durango, enjoying an active retirement of 21 years.

**Roderick E. Barker** Rod took over the "reins" of the Strater in 1983. Initially, for the first two years, he served as Property Manager directing the backlog of renovation work at the Strater. In 1985, Rod filled the position of General Manager where for the past 24 years, he has been overseeing and managing all of the hotel's affairs being Owner, President and CEO of the Strater Corporation. Rod was also active in the Colorado Hotel and Lodging Association, serving as its president in 1989. He was named Hotelier of the Year in 1991. In 1993, he was appointed by Governor Romer, to serve on the Colorado Tourism Board thru 2000, including two years as Chairman. He received the Chancellor's Tourism Award for Leadership and service, University of Colorado in 1993 and the Distinguished Alumni Award, Fort Lewis College in 1999. He helped found the Association of Historic Hotels of the Rocky Mountain West, and was one of 10 founding members of the National Trust's Historic Hotels of America. It has been Rod's insight that has raised the Strater to the level of elegance and beauty that she has today.

# 1926—2009 The Barker's Take the Reins

As you might expect, the work is never done at the Strater. The Strater employs a large fulltime staff to keep up with the demands of its 93 guest rooms and 68,000 square foot facility. Much attention was paid to the environmental impacts of the hotel and the Strater leads the way in its efforts to reduce its carbon footprint. In the late 1980's, Rod and a local engineer created a way to capture the waste heat created by the air-conditioning system and reclaim that heat into a 5,000 gallon hot water storage tank stored in a vault below the ground, to provide all the hot water for the hotels guests during the summer season. That process is still working today and many hours are spent to find new efficient ways to heat and cool the building to reduce the carbon footprint. New windows are being installed to reduce heating and cooling demands and high efficiency boilers are being reviewed to bring the efficiencies of those systems into a commercial application. The Victorians were very advanced in their application of technology and Rod and his staff are still embracing forward thinking technology to make the 120 year-old hotel run like a state of the art facility.

With the tradition of adding new improvements to the hotel each year, the hotel began giving an annual Open House to show the residents of the Durango community, what new things had happened in "Their" hotel. The Annual Open House is held on the third Thursday of April and the entire community is always invited. Rod and his staff realized that their future rested in the commitment of the locals to promote the hotel and it was important to make sure that they were able to see the rooms and the renovations that were done each year. During the period of 1987 to 2009, there has been an average of 500 people attending the open house each year. Many of Durango's History Buffs are involved in a group called "Mrs. Camp's Town Ladies and Gents". They dress up in vintage Victorian and "Turn-of-the-Century" costumes and help to make the affair more festive. It is a big party and a big success for everyone. The Strater Hotel truly is Durango's Hotel and the "Jewel of the Rockies".

There is no doubt that the future hold many new and exciting changes for the Strater, but the factors that brought the hotel through 122 years of history are many, its staff has stood for friendly hospitality, fun entertainment, quality craftsmanship and a genuine reflection of the colorful history of Durango and the Old West. So, as you walk thru the lobby, sip a drink in the Diamond Belle Saloon or Office Spiritorium; dine in the elegant Mahogany Grille, or check into one of the beautiful Victorian rooms, you can't help but connect with the likes of writer Louis L'Amour, pioneer Otto Mears, photographer William Jackson, Presidents John F. Kennedy and Gerald Ford, Astronaut Stewart Roosa, oil man Peter Groth, banker Tom Sefton, director Renny Harlan and actor Chevy Chase. Be a part of history and notice the difference it makes in your life. You'll be glad you did!

The Strater stands with all of its glory today because of the vision of the Barker family. They have been the only family to both own and manage this gemstone in the Rockies. In doing so they have been able to maintain the control and provide the tender loving care that is required in order to keep the Strater flourishing. Starting with Earl Barker Sr. in 1926, his son Earl following him in 1968 and then Rod in 1983, the Barker family has been "at the reins" of the Strater for some eighty-three years at the time of this writing.

The following chapter will provide a photo tour of the hotel showcasing the beauty and dignity of the Strater.

# Chapter Six
## 6

# Photo Tour of the Strater Hotel

# Photo Tour of the Strater Hotel

*The experience of the Strater* comes close to traveling back in time. From the moment you step through the ornate front doors, your senses are overwhelmed with an aristocratic beauty from bygone days. It is hoped that the photos in this chapter give you a foretaste of the beauty and superb eloquence one experiences when they stay at the Strater Hotel in Durango, Colorado.

*The front entrance of the Strater includes display cases filled with items that would have been found in a quality hotel in the 1880's. Directly past the display cases and to the right as you enter, hangs the original mailbox for the Strater, still in use to this day.*

# Photo Tour of the Strater Hotel

*Both photos present the tasteful décor of the front lobby as you enter the Strater.*

# Photo Tour of the Strater Hotel

***The Lobby Front Desk***—The political term "lobbying" comes from the days when citizens would meet their congressmen and senators in the lobbies of grand hotels such as the Strater. Hotel lobbies were historically quite often the social gathering place of the residents and where most people congregated. The Strater lobby was like a stock exchange for the mining industry. Day and night, men were engaged here in the lobby in rapid fire discussions about the silver issue, which greatly affected the entire economy of the San Juan Basin. The Strater Lobby was designed and renovated by Rod Barker in 1996. The original Cleveland Safe built in 1887 is still housed in the Strater front office and is still in use today bearing the name, "Strater House". The back part of the front desk shown here is an antique walnut buffet. The carving in the buffet above and center is of the Greek god Bacchus or Dionysus, son of Zeus. Dionysus is the god of wine, fertility, joyous living and hospitality. The Barkers felt that this home was a fitting place for the walnut piece including the carving. The beautiful chandeliers are from the old Durango Courthouse, which was torn down.

*The cherry reception desk shown here was constructed by master craftsman Charlie Schumacher. The gentleman behind the desk is Rick Douesnard. He was the kind person that gave me my first tour, when I entered the Strater for the first time in 2006.*

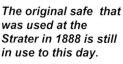

*The original safe that was used at the Strater in 1888 is still in use to this day.*

*The solid cast doors on the safe are 10 inches thick and weigh an estimated 300 lbs. each!*

134

# Photo Tour of the Strater Hotel

After checking in at the front desk, you then proceed into this corridor up to the stairway that has been in use since the hotel's opening day. Or you might decide to take the modern Otis elevator which is located across from the stairway, under the leaded glass ornamental overhang. As you approach the landing of the stairway, you come upon an appealing parlor properly named the "Back Lobby." This was another meeting area in the early Strater days. The "Back Lobby" was designed by Rod Barker to be a formal sitting area. It also features wireless internet access for guests. The gorgeous marble fireplace came from France.

# Photo Tour of the Strater Hotel

**The Diamond Belle**—The Strater hotel's original saloon was named the Strater Bar. Opening in 1888, when the hotel was brand new, it lasted until the early 1900's. Then, Turner Investments overhauled the room and it became their offices, followed by the Silver State Security Companies, and then the Colorado Employment Agency. In 1957, Earl Barker Jr. and Bob Blomstrom restored the room back to a turn of the century saloon calling it the Diamond Belle. The costumes of the bar staff and the ragtime piano entertainment are reminiscent of that bygone era. Several of the costumes from years past are displayed above the bar.

# Photo Tour of the Strater Hotel

**The Office Spiritorium -** Originally built in 1881 by the Strater Brothers, this room was originally their Paints and Oils Store. By the late 1880's the room had been renovated into a barber shop. When the Columbian hotel was built in 1893, enveloping this structure, this room became the Columbian Hotel's lobby. The Columbian and Strater hotels merged into the one Strater in 1902, at which time the room was reverted back into a barber shop, lasting nearly six decades. Then in the 1960's, it was again renovated into a private club for the area oil and gas executives and named the Durango Petroleum Club. The next change came in the 1970's, when the room became one of the Strater's banquet rooms—the Columbian Room. The present day Office Spiritorium was designed and built by Rod Barker in the year 2000. Every detail of the room was included in this makeover including the furniture, walls and balcony. Even the chairs were made by the Strater staff. The chandelier was found thanks to the internet, and came from a wealthy resident living in Beverly Hills, CA. The lush furniture, antique typewriters, bottles and artifacts from much earlier years in Durango, add to the cozy atmosphere that is accentuated by the lavish hand-carved fireplace.

# Photo Tour of the Strater Hotel

**The Mahogany Grille -** Originally, this room was the Opera House of the Columbian Hotel. Henry Strater's wife was a concert pianist and would perform here for guests. Now the hotel's restaurant, the Mahogany Grille, offers a casual atmosphere decorated with elegant mahogany, Tiffany style domes, Bradbury & Bradbury Art Wallpapers, a Mason-Hamlin Symetrigrand piano and an exposed brick wall of the original Columbian Hotel, dating back to 1893.

The room has undergone several name and design changes over the years; some may remember it as the Red Lantern Inn; the Strater Coffee Shop; the Terrace Dining Room; the Opera House Dining Room and most recently, Henry's Chophouse.

# Photo Tour of the Strater Hotel

*Georgio Polacco*
*04/12/1873—04/30/1960*

*The beautiful antique buffet in the Mahogany Grille features mirrored glass panels behind the vase that lift up from behind. This was designed so that the prepared food could be served from the preparation area in the home into the dining room by the servers on staff without being seen.*

*The mirrored buffet was originally in the home of Maestro Arturo Toscanini in Italy.*

*It was brought from Milan, Italy by the Metropolitan and European opera star, Edith Mason and her husband Georgio Polacco, who followed Toscanini as conductor at the Metropolitan Opera.*

*Edith Mason*
*03/22/1892—11/26/1973*

*In 1920, George Polacco became the conductor of the Chicago Opera where he was conductor for many years. Miss Mason appeared with world renowned Opera greats including Caruso and Pinza and was coached for her role in Madame Butterfly by Puccini himself.*

139

# Photo Tour of the Strater Hotel

**The Oak Room** - This is a banquet/meeting room for private parties and an auxiliary area for the Mahogany Grille in high seasons. The unique wallpaper is set off by wood wainscoting with built in display cases. Stained glass over a gas fireplace adds a warm atmosphere and creates ambiance to other original artwork displayed on the walls.

# Photo Tour of the Strater Hotel

Attention to detail is evident throughout the Strater. Even the staircase to the lower level is simply beautiful. No area has been overlooked by Rod Barker, the driving force and visionary of the Strater Hotel today.

# Photo Tour of the Strater Hotel

**The Pullman Room -** used to be called the Gold Room. If only these walls could speak! It was in this room that presidential nominee John F. Kennedy delivered his 1960 campaign address. This was also the location for the historic signing of TAT-6, the Trans-Atlantic Treaty #6 for the laying of the Trans-Atlantic communications cable. [1]

The Pullman Room was completely redesigned in 1987 and is fashioned in the style of a plush Pullman railroad car of the 1800's. The authenticity of the décor is accented by crystal chandeliers and custom mirrors. The Persian style carpet was custom designed and crafted for this room. Shadow boxes containing collectibles of the by-gone era line the wall. Concealed within the Victorian elegance is "state-of-the art" multi media technology. This ballroom while large, has an intimate home-like atmosphere and has seating for up to 128 guests, banquet style.

*[1] For details and photos of John F. Kennedy's stay at the Strater along with details and photos of TAT-6, see Chapter 9—"Who Slept In My Bed."*

# Photo Tour of the Strater Hotel

**The Centennial Room -** was at one time the location of the Nugget Bar, also called The Snake Pit. The Centennial Room serves as a conference room as well as a buffet room to the Pullman for large dinner parties. Pictures on display recognize Marion Jarvis, Jentra Barker's mother, when she was honored as Durango's Centennial Queen in 1981. Louis L'Amour, President Ford and Mayor Fred Kroeger were honored dignitaries at this event. The Centennial Room is designed in the Arts and Crafts Era style. It is an elegant setting for a family dinner or a business retreat.

# Photo Tour of the Strater Hotel

**The First Floor**

**Room 108 -** is the largest sleeping room in the hotel. Originally, in 1888, the hotel dining room was located in this room along with the current Sales and Catering office next door. The wallpaper, designed by Christopher Dresser, is circa 1875. The top of the bar was found in an old garage and the hotel's renowned craftsman, Charles Schumacher, matched the bottom.

# Photo Tour of the Strater Hotel

## The Second Floor

As you exit the elevator, or take the stairs to the second floor, you can't help but notice that attention has been given to every detail. The furniture, lighting, choice of furniture and wall paper all add to feeling that you have entered a luxury hotel in the 1800's. On my initial visit to the Strater, I was walking up the stairs to my room. Suddenly, my ears were filled with the "chug-chug" of the coal fired steam locomotive powering up, as the 1920's vintage train was leaving the train station and "chugging" by, directly behind the Strater. At that moment, I felt as if I had literally stepped back in time.

# Photo Tour of the Strater Hotel

**Room 220** - is an award winner, taking one of the top three prestigious "International Gold Key Awards" in 1989. Note the "antique" corner armoire designed by Rod Barker and made by Charlie Schumacher out of walnut and mahogany. Construction is the old style with tongue and groove joints. The Victorian furniture in this room came from the Carlsbad, New Mexico area.

# Photo Tour of the Strater Hotel

**Room 222 -** was reserved for an entire month each summer for many years by Western author Louis L'Amour and his family. Mr. L'Amour enjoyed being in the center of Durango activities. From his vantage point in this room, he could watch the Fiesta parades and all the street activity, while getting inspiration from the strains of the Honky Tonk Piano floating up from the Diamond Belle Saloon, just below. He did a great deal of his writing here, in room 222.

# Photo Tour of the Strater Hotel

**Room 226 -** is furnished in Russian Gothic. This was the first room in the Strater to receive a complete set of Bradbury & Bradbury Wall Paper. Each color requires a "Stencil" impression which is applied by hand. An average sized Victorian home can require 1,000 impressions. Can you begin to imagine the number required for the Strater's 93 rooms as well as public locations?

# Photo Tour of the Strater Hotel

**Room 227 -** is one of the Strater Honeymoon suites. Note the four piece matching set of furniture. This 19th century Eastlake* set was discovered at a dilapidating plantation, located in Montgomery, Alabama. The plantation was originally built in the 1850's by a cotton grower named Archibald Pitt Tyson. The furniture had been in the Tyson family home since the mid to late 1800's. The home had been locked up and untouched for 20 years up until 1977.

In 1977, the decision was made to renovate the home and turn it into a Bed & Breakfast Restaurant. The furnishings in the home were being auctioned off. Fortunately, Earl and Jentra Barker were able to purchase this beautiful furniture. Today this four piece set has a value of over $100,000. When you combine this furniture with the Bradbury & Bradbury wallpaper and then add the plush purple velvet draperies, you have a room that is simply gorgeous!

*The Eastlake furniture style as envisioned by its namesake, Charles Lock Eastlake, came about in response to his dislike of the over-the-top Rococo and Renaissance Revival styles popular during the Victorian era. Although Eastlake furniture is technically considered Victorian, being popular from 1870-1890, it breaks away from the excessive high relief carving, classical elements and numerous curves of other styles produced during this timeframe.[55]*

# Photo Tour of the Strater Hotel

The fully restored Tyson home is on the National Register of Historic Homes in Lowndesboro, located 15 miles west of Montgomery, Alabama.

# Photo Tour of the Strater Hotel

**Room 233 -** is the Governors suite. Since the 1890's, all of Colorado's governors have stayed at the Strater Hotel, and the most recent have stayed in this room.

# Photo Tour of the Strater Hotel

**Third Floor** - View looking down over the balcony from the third floor.

# Photo Tour of the Strater Hotel

**Room 322 -** is one of several honeymoon suites. This is the bed originally found in Atlanta, GA. by Jentra Barker in 1963, that started the Victorian renovation process and the beginning of the Strater American Victorian Antique furniture collection; the largest collection in the world! The top of the tester was stuffed with Spanish moss under China Silk. Note the Eastlake design.

The bed was originally manufactured in New Orleans – circa 1860. Prior to the Civil War, the bed was shipped to Vicksburg on the Mississippi River and then used in a mansion along the river. There are seven different wallpapers in room 322, at a cost of over $3,000.

# Photo Tour of the Strater Hotel

**Room 323 -** has special significance because this is the room where Gustaf Nordenskiold was held under house arrest, in 1891. He arrest became an international issue. This is detailed in Chapter 9, "Who Slept In My Bed." The sofa was once located in the Kentucky Governor's Mansion.

# Photo Tour of the Strater Hotel

**Room 327 -** Note the beautiful 3 piece Eastlake set, and the interior style, one of the two rooms in the hotel with exposed brick and cedar wood paneling.

# Photo Tour of the Strater Hotel

**Room 333 -** is the Presidential Suite. President Gerald Ford stayed in this room during the 1970's and again in 1996. In 1996 the room was renovated, including the elaborate ceiling woodwork handcrafted by the Strater's own woodshop. Also note the 24 karat gold wall paper.

# Photo Tour of the Strater Hotel

**Fourth Floor, Room 422 -** was J.A. Segerberg's living quarters. Mr. Segerberg was hired to manage the hotel in 1929. He held the position of part owner and general manager for twenty years. This room was renovated in 1993. The wall paper is Bradbury and Bradbury, authentic reproduction. The ceiling style is called "Cracked Ice".

# Photo Tour of the Strater Hotel

**Room 423 -** is special, in that this was Earl Barker Seniors bed. The netting was originally fish net (now it's lace) which was purchased by the pound. The window treatments are Austrian Shades.

# Photo Tour of the Strater Hotel

**Room 424 -** was renovated in 1993. It is decorated with Neo-Greco wallpaper along with velvet draperies costing over $3,000.

# Photo Tour of the Strater Hotel

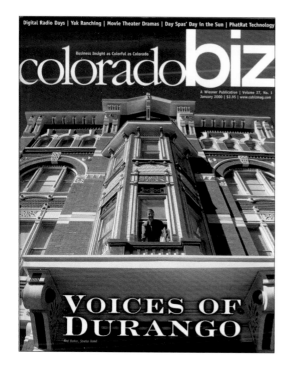

The "Colorado Biz" Magazine ran a feature article on the Strater including this great cover photo of the Strater with Rod looking out of the window. This was the January 2000 issue.

The National Lodging Magazine issue of February 1989 also ran a feature article, with the Strater on the cover. The writer, Ken Koepper stated, *"This is no ordinary small hotel. Most properties with hundreds of rooms can't match the Strater in terms of guest experience."*

Jerrol Boyer, The American Hotel and Motel Association Director of Smaller Property Services stated, *"It's the only place I know where you know every minute that something unusual is going to happen."*

It is not surprising to read comments the likes of those above. Reviewing the previous pages, you have experienced a sampling of the rooms. No two rooms are alike! The Strater has the largest collection of American Victorian walnut furniture in the world, offering 93 impeccably appointed Victorian rooms. In addition to this unmatchable collection, the hand-screened Bradbury & Bradbury wallpapers; as well as the countless antiques and artifacts, compliment the Strater with elegance and beauty far beyond one's expectations. Chapter nine entitled *"Strater's Historical Treasures"* showcase a number of these antiques and artifacts.

One afternoon in June of 2007 while walking near the Durango Train Depot, I happened upon a kind gentleman named Russell Steel. He was an artist selling his work at a stand that he had set up. When I saw this watercolor of the Strater along with the musing written below, I fell in love with it and knew that I would have a place for this art in my book. Mr. Steel was 89 years old when I met him. He told me that he loved Durango and had been a citizen here since the 1950's. Rusty, thank you for this beautiful watercolor and also your wit.

# Chapter Seven
## 7

# Charlie Schumacher
# The Master Craftsman

# Charlie Schumacher—The Master Craftsman

*By this point in the book,* I hope that you will agree with me in saying that the Strater Hotel is a treasure that has captured our hearts. You have witnessed through the turning of the pages, the many stages of the Strater's history. From its infancy, when all that the rooms had was a bed, a commode and a pot belly stove; to the lean years when the hotel stood aging, still beautiful and elegant, but pleading for someone to offer their tender loving care. With the proper help, she could be restored to her rightful position as the "Jewel of the Rockies".

Thankfully, the Barkers stepped up to the plate. Rod's grandfather and then his father took care of the essentials during their stewardship, making sure that the structure and the utilities were updated and modernized. A monumental task!

When Rod accepted the stewardship of the Strater, he recognized and more than that, he appreciated the unique beauty and splendor of the Strater that had been entrusted to him. His parents, Earl and Jentra had already begun restoring the Victorian charm by conducting an ongoing search for the authentic American Victorian walnut furniture. When Rod took over, he picked up this torch as well, but with an enthusiasm and passion that only comes from a person who has a deep love for what he does. He has without a doubt put his heart and soul into the Strater.

Having this passion-this love, as well as the foresight to elevate the Strater into the magnificent structure that it is today, would not be possible without the ability to transform ideas into tangible reality. It is an awesome gift to be able to visualize an idea or picture in a way that you would like for a room to look. To bring that picture into reality, requires the skill and craftsmanship of a Master.

The Barkers have been blessed with the privilege of becoming friends with and employing perhaps one of the finest wood craftsman alive today, Mr. Charlie Schumacher. I say this with total sincerity! True I am no carpenter, however I did specialize in wood working all four years in high school. In my senior year, there were no "Woods" classes left to take, so they actually made up a class for me, so that I could have another year at what I enjoyed most - woodworking. It was my "Pipe Dream" to become a Master Carpenter making furniture. This didn't materialize, but I have never lost my appreciation for the quality and the craftsmanship that goes into fine furniture and woodworking in general. So Charlie, you're a hero in my eyes!

Charlie Schumacher has been working on the Strater for longer than most of us have been alive. He loves the Strater and he loves Durango. I had the privilege of spending time with him and also interviewing him, and now I too call Charlie my friend. Here is his story:

*"I was born on November 18, 1927 right here in Durango. I have lived in this town my entire life. I started working for my father when I was ten years old. My father hired me to hang wall paper and paid me fifty cents a day. I could hang wall paper faster and better than most. I had more money than I could spend, I even bought my own bicycle."*

*"I did other jobs as well. I remember when my brother and I painted the Animas City School House* (Which today houses the Animas City Museum). *They had a 44 foot extension ladder to paint the outside, but it wasn't tall enough, so we went and bolted half of a 36 foot extension ladder onto the top of it making it a 62 foot ladder! We climbed to the top of that ladder and it was funny because the ladder had a HUGE bend in the middle".*

# Charlie Schumacher—The Master Craftsman

Charlie started working with wood in the fourth grade, making little wooden gadgets. *"Then I took Shop all through high school, including a half-year of mechanical drawing."* Before Charlie could begin furniture making in school, he had to pass a test imposed by his Shop teacher. Charlie said that his shop teacher *"got the tip of a lead pencil as sharp as he could, then drew a straight line down a board. `When you can rip it so, half the line is on the board and the other half in the sawdust pile, you're ready to build furniture' was the way he put it."* Charlie accomplished this in the tenth grade.

*"With the assistance of my two brothers, we built all the furniture for my folk's house out of solid walnut; all hand done, no machinery."*

Charlie told me that he has been all over the Strater on steel scaffolding that measures just five foot by seven foot. He jokes that *"Today, nobody will even climb that scaffolding."* Well, without a doubt Charlie is fearless, that's all that I can say.

Charlie spent 1-1/2 years in the Service during World War II. Upon his return from the Service and back to Durango, he and his brother purchased his father's paint business. Unfortunately for Charlie, after twenty-five years of making and using lead paint, he was suffering from lead paint poisoning. He was having stomach problems, his gums were turning purple and his teeth were falling out. So, he got out of the paint business.

It has been so long, he doesn't remember when it was, that he first started working on the Strater with the Barkers. When he first started, he worked for Earl Barker Sr. The first job he had was painting the dining room where today we have the Mahogany Grille. Charlie said that *"Earl Sr. wanted the room all painted with white enamel. He wanted it painted between midnight and eight in the morning. He didn't want to lose any business."* He couldn't recall what year this was, but knows that it was before 1956, when it was called the Coffee Shop.

He also did the work on the Diamond Belle Saloon some 50 years ago. He escorted me into the Diamond Belle and pointed out the "Marble Pillars" located in the second level balcony. He said, *"They're wood painted to look like marble. I did this with a process using turkey feathers."*

He went onto say: *"The whole world has changed today. You go to the store and buy a special primer for a stain or something. My Granddaddy used to go to the slaughterhouse with a gallon bucket and he would get blood from a slaughtered animal and*

# Charlie Schumacher—The Master Craftsman

*that killed the stain right away. He would paint the blood over the stain, let that dry and then he could paint over it and the stain would not bleed through...... It's the same with gold leaf, my granddaddy used to use egg whites to glue gold leaf on."*

Charlie Schumacher is from the "Old School". He was taught by those who were "Old School" when he was young. He recalls his grandfather buying white lead by the 100 pound keg. *"We'd break it up and mix linseed oil, turpentine, and pigment with it to get a flat paint. For enamel, we'd add varnish to the mix. Then, if you wanted to flatten back the enamel, you'd add a ball of beeswax. Yep, beeswax– a ball about the size of a walnut thinned to liquid with turpentine added to a gallon of paint."*[47] Old School—no question about it!

Because of this, Charlie Schumacher has been able to do amazing feats at the Strater that are authentic, and completed in the same way and fashion as they would have been done back in 1887, when the hotel was brand new. That is of course, with the exception of the lead paint!

The changes that the Strater has experienced during the last 50 years have been done under the guidance and skilled hands of Charlie Schumacher. He spoke to me about the time that he was remodeling twelve rooms on the second and third floors back in the 1960's. Prior to that time, the rooms had been used for truckers that stayed at the Strater in those days. He was in the process of taking six rooms on each floor, that up until that time simply had a bed, a chair and a small sink in them, and doubling their size. The six rooms became three rooms. Today this area includes the Governor's Suite. It was during this major remodeling project that he found some records going back to the turn of the past century that showed that they were charging only fifty cents per night!

Charlie also took me into another room, The Office Spiritorium. He was the craftsman behind all the beautiful work in this room as well.

The décor and beauty of this room was a vision in Rod Barker's mind. It was Charlie that brought it to fruition. When Rod found this black & white photo of a railing in a magazine, he asked Charlie; *"Can you make this for the Office?"* Of course, with Charlie, when it comes to working with wood, the word "No" does not exist! Compare the black & white photo to Charlie's finished work on the next page. You can now appreciate, when I called him "one of the finest wood craftsman alive," I wasn't exaggerating.

# Charlie Schumacher—The Master Craftsman

When Charlie was preparing to build this staircase, he had a concern; Being made out of wood, if someone was to accidently fall against it, he knew that the wood might give. This could cause grave injury to someone. To satisfy this concern, he reinforced the entire upper railing with a steel frame and then enclosed the steel frame with the beautiful woodwork.

# Charlie Schumacher—The Master Craftsman

The beautiful fireplace in the Office Spiritorium is Charlie's work, as is the solid cherry front desk in the Strater Lobby. Regarding "The Office" fireplace, Charlie said: *"I built it in my garage, mirrors and all."*

Wherever you go in the Strater today, you can be certain that Charlie has been there and that the beautiful wood work you see throughout is the result of his gift.

As of the writing of this book in 2009, Charlie is 82 years old and in active retirement. When I was in Durango in January of 2009, he was still on hand to offer his expertise and advice. During my January stay, the elevator was being renovated. Charlie was called upon because of his knowledge and experience with all the idiosyncrasies of the stately Strater.

Charlie Schumacher—thank you for a job well done!

# Charlie Schumacher—The Master Craftsman

For a person that has been so active throughout his life, you may wonder—what is Charlie doing now? Well, even though he is 82 years old, he is living testimony to the statement that "you're never too old to learn something new"!

About two years ago Charlie took up painting watercolors. His "magic hands" went to work on the "canvas" and just like the woodworking, he is turning out masterpieces! The quality of his work is so good, that it could probably be marketed and sold commercially.

Here are a few of his pieces including his watercolor of the Strater Hotel on the next page.

# Charlie Schumacher—The Master Craftsman

*Watercolor of the Strater Hotel—Painted by Charlie Schumacher*

# Chapter Eight
## 8

# Strater's Historical Treasures

# Strater's Historical Treasures

*The Strater* has appropriately been designated a "museum". With the breadth and depth of its antiques and Victorian furniture, this is a fitting classification. The following pages display a number of these precious and rare items.

**The Ladies Reading Club** Banquet Program dated May 28, 1895 is shown here. The original ribbon used to attach the brochure is still intact.

The Reading Club of Durango was established in 1882. In 1894 it became one of the first federated Women's Clubs in Colorado. Its membership is limited to 25 members. Throughout its history, its members have represented some of the most influential families in Durango. The Reading Club is still active today in 2009, without any interruption in its 127 year history.

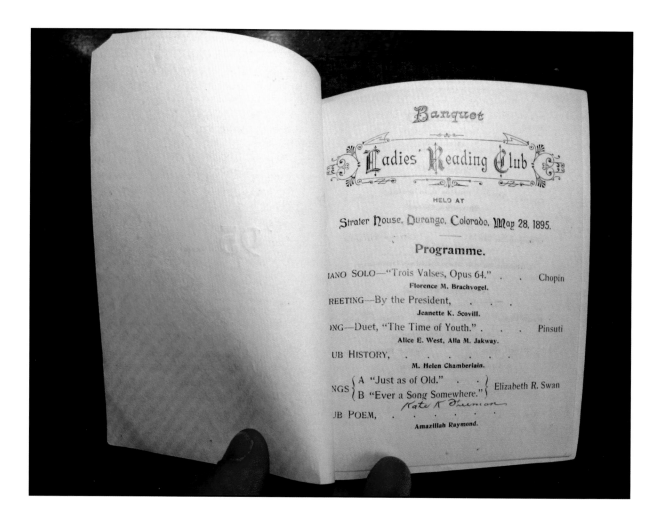

# Strater's Historical Treasures

Tucked away in a bookcase in the inviting "Back Lobby" is a one page menu, originally called a "Bill of Fare." This document originated from the famous Delmonico Restaurants of New York. [57]

The Delmonico Restaurants of New York are famous for a number of reasons. The first and foremost is that the Delmonico family opened the first restaurant in the United States in the early 1830's. Up until this time, inns served the same meal to everyone. There was no choice and everyone paid the same amount, whether they ate a lot or little. The Delmonicos followed the example of restaurants in Paris and offered patrons a choice. The menu shown below is from the second restaurant that they opened on Pearl Street, the first being at 23 and 25 William Street. The family opened up a number of restaurants (Ten in all) in New York. The last of the original Delmonico Restaurants closed its doors in 1923.

This Menu from 1834, originally called a "Bill of Fare," was the first printed American "Bill Of Fare" in the country. The word "menu" was not coined until 1835. The Bill of Fare offers a 'regular dinner' at 12 cents and lists a hamburger steak at 10 cents (the same price as roast chicken or ham and eggs; regular beef steak is only 4 cents, as are pork chops, corn beef and cabbage and fried fish. Roast beef or veal, roast mutton, veal cutlet, or chicken stew are 5 cents).

*In the early 1830's, the cost of a hamburger (10 cents) was double that of a Veal Cutlet (5 cents)*

*The Aetna Petroleum Corporation stocks shown here are dated March 9th, 1921. The shareholder had purchased 14 shares at Five dollars each.*

*The irons show two variations. The iron to the right is a simple cast iron flat iron. It has a #6 imprinted on the top designating its weight—six pounds. The iron to the left has a small tank for fuel. Some used natural gas, others kerosene, alcohol, whale oil or even gasoline. It's hard to imagine ironing with a burning flame inside an iron, but these liquid fuel irons were sold to rural families well into the twentieth century. The liquid fuel sometimes caught on fire, singed the handle, or simply exploded.*

*The Singer Child's working sewing machine dates to circa 1910.*

# Strater's Historical Treasures

*Dating back to the turn of the century, this Blackberry pattern shaving mug has been in Laurie Barker's family for generations. It is on display in the front lobby with soap, brush and mirror set. The brush, such as this shown in the photo, commonly used boar bristle. The handles were made from a variety of sources including ivory, porcelain, silver, gold or wood.*

*O·sa·to Tonic—"Beneficial in Liver and Kidney Troubles" was manufactured by the Manhattan Medicine Company. This product was sold as a laxative. The Manhattan Medicine Company was established in 1877 in Des Moines, Iowa.*

*Various Indian tribes have made the San Juan Valley and surrounding area their home for thousands of years. The hand made bow and moccasins date back to the 19th century.*

# Strater's Historical Treasures

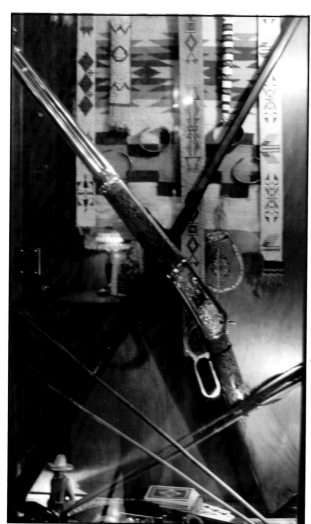

This display case contains items that are from Rod Barker's personal collection. The Winchester 30/30 on display is a model 94 referring to the date of 1894 when the model was designed by Browning who worked for Winchester. This particular rifle was made by Winchester arms in Cheyenne and is a La Plata County Commemorative. Engravings in 24 Caret gold include the Strater, the Durango Railroad Station, the Courthouse and Mesa Verde. Winchester had intended to manufacture and sell 20 of these unique rifles at a price of $6,000 dollars each, but could not get orders for the minimum number. So Rod Barker purchased the "proof". Because of these developments, this rifle is the only one of its kind.

The rifle behind the Winchester is a Frank Wesson 32 RF (Rim Fire). His brother, Daniel Wesson was the co-founder of Smith and Wesson. Daniel's baby brother Frank started his own firearms manufacturing firm in 1859.

The Colt handgun in the case is a 32-20 Colt peacemaker. It dates back to 1907. The firearms in this display case are on rotation. At times other pieces may be on display.

*Women's apparel was very ornate at the turn of the century. Examples of hair pins, jewelry, and hand bags are shown here.*

# Strater's Historical Treasures

*Beautiful glassware such as this is on display at the Strater.*

*Displays by Laurie Barker*

*Note the quality, craftsmanship and detail that went into products 100 plus years ago. The quality of the leather boots, the beauty of the handle on the shoe brush, the engraved handles on the tweezers and other small tools, as well as even the simple silk page marker wrapped around the book with an inscription dated 1892, are all examples of a lost art that has occurred due in large part to mass production. The Strater "Museum" aids all who stop and ponder over her treasures, to appreciate how life has changed over the past 100 years.*

# Strater's Historical Treasures

*Collection of Frank and Ricci Dawson*

*This particular display had a unique and powerful impact in my heart, my inner being………..*

*As I reviewed this photo, I was reflecting upon the "relics" on display. I thought about the people that were personally influenced by these items;*

*The man or woman that wore the spectacles;*
*The bride and groom in the photo, dated August 09, 1923, along with the wedding invitation just behind it;*
*The young lady in the photograph;*
*The man who used to shave with the quality shaving brush to the right*
*or the straight razor in the picture frame.*

*They no longer walk this earth. Articles that once belonged to them are now here, on display.*
*I thought to myself: "Our lives go by so quickly!"*

*We are the recipient of memories of events that we encounter. In time, we too become but a memory to someone else who encountered us. Once these persons pass on and become memories of others themselves as we will have, the memory of us is all but lost, except for a possible photo or a memoir that we may have written.*

*True, death is a part of life that we all share and will experience. This is not negative, this is normal and natural. However, by taking time to reflect on displays such as the photo shown here, it helps me to appreciate the importance of living life to the fullest, and living in the now! The day will come when I too will be just a distant memory or remembered by a photograph on display in an antique display case.*

*This is one of the reasons why I am so motivated and passionate about gathering information and photographing locations, and then taking time to research and bring the results together in a volume such as this for people to enjoy. I have seen first hand, that books such as this have an ability to help people to sit back and reflect on the past. People are able to take their mind off of their own "universe" so to speak, with its complexities and hectic pace of life, and widen out and see life from a different perspective.*

*I personally value the importance of doing this. It assists me in more fully appreciating the preciousness of life, to "stop and smell the roses" and value even the simple things in life.*

# Strater's Historical Treasures

*Display by Jentra Barker*

*This showcase is adorned with hair pins and sales aids illustrating elegant apparel dating back to 1890 from Madrid, Spain. The heirloom (lower right) is an ashtray! The baby's mouth is the location for the cigarettes or cigars.*

*(Note the mirror in the small photo to the left)*

*These bottles of liquor on display in the Mahogany Grille from Charles E. Stilwell, date back to the days of Prohibition that began in 1920 and ran until 1933. During those years the sale, manufacture, and transportation of alcohol for consumption were banned nationally as mandated in the Eighteenth Amendment to the United States Constitution.*

*The illegal production and distribution of liquor or bootlegging, became rampant and the national government did not have the means or desire to enforce every border, lake, river, and speakeasy in America. In fact, by 1925 in New York City alone, there were anywhere from 30,000 to 100,000 speakeasy clubs.*

*The same held true for Durango. There were numerous sources of alcohol available in this area as well. The bottles shown here are part of the Greg Stilwell Collection. His grandfather ran the Strater Hotel from 1896 up into the early 1920's. As stated earlier in chapter five, the Strater also had a resource for attending to peoples' desire for alcohol. Johnny McNamara worked as a bellhop at the Strater during his younger years. During the Prohibition era, he hid bootleg liquor under the elevator. Of course, this was not condoned by the Strater management nor did they even have knowledge of this at the time. (So they say!)*

*When Earl Barker Sr. took over the ownership of the Strater in 1926, Prohibition was still in effect. He was certainly relieved when this came to an end. Within a short period after its culmination, he ordered an entire train car load of Early Times Whiskey! That is equivalent to four semi trucks of whiskey. As you can tell, he never wanted to run out again!*[48]

*The Strater Hotel is on record as being the longest running Early Times customer as well as one of the largest, in all of Colorado.*

# Strater's Historical Treasures

*Thomas Edison's work on two other inventions, the telegraph and the telephone led to his development of the original phonograph.*

*In 1877 Edison was working on a machine that would transcribe telegraphic messages through indentations on paper tape, which could later be sent over the telegraph repeatedly. This development led Edison to speculate that a telephone message could also be recorded in a similar fashion. He experimented with a diaphragm which had an embossing point and was held against rapidly moving paraffin paper. The speaking vibrations made indentations in the paper. Edison later changed the paper to a metal cylinder with tin foil wrapped around it.*

*The machine shown here and on display at the Strater (color photo) is one of the early model phonographs with the metal cylinder.*

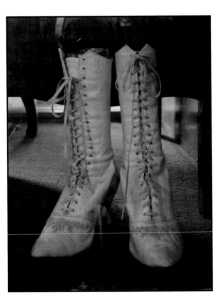

*These were Laurie Barker's Great Grandmother's wedding shoes. Her Great Grandmother, Marie Prince Moore was wed back in 1891. These are on display in the front lobby.*

*The kerosene lamp to the right dates back to the Civil War era. It was purchased in the 1940's by Laurie's Barker's grandparents, Lynn and Truman Moore, from an antique store in Louisiana. It is on display in the front lobby.*

# Strater's Historical Treasures

The Blickensderfer Typewriter was designed by George C. Blickensderfer (1850-1917) in 1893. It was originally intended to compete with Remington desk typewriters, but ended up being known for its portability. Blickensderfer's typewriter contained only 250 parts compared to the 2,500 parts of a standard typewriter. Therefore, it was much smaller, lighter, and cheaper than the desk typewriters. It also featured a type wheel that was easily removed to change the typeface.

The typewriter on display at the Strater is a Model No. 6. which was released in 1906. The *Blick 6* was in fact a *Blick 5*, with an aluminum frame. This is notable because the *Blick 5* was introduced at the 1893 World's Columbian Exposition in Chicago. The *Blick 5* was one of the first truly portable typewriters with a full keyboard. The *Blick 6*, having an aluminum frame made it even lighter for portability.

# Chapter Nine
## 9

# Who Slept In My Bed?

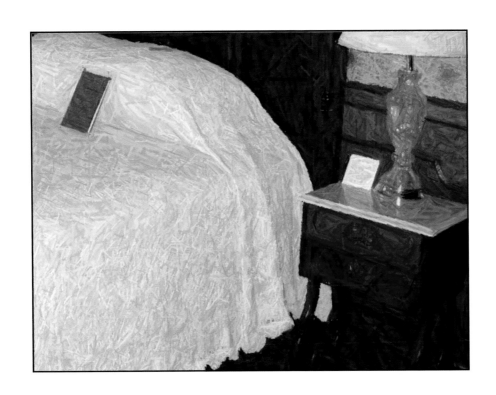

# Who Slept in My Bed?

*A stay at the Strater is a great experience!* The charm and character of the hotel reaches out and wraps it's arms around your heart. Extra little touches truly make your stay at the Strater a memory that won't be quickly forgotten.

On my first stay at the Strater in October of 2006, I stayed in Room 418. Upon entering my room for the first time, I was impressed with the comfort and warmth that this room held. The cheery white bed spread, the beautiful dark wood headboard, the wicker furniture.... everything was just right.

As I laid my suitcase down, I immediately noticed a small red book resting against one of my pillows. I sat down on my queen size bed and opened the cover to find that this was a "Room Diary." I had never seen this before! As I browsed through the pages, I was impressed with the fact that people from all walks of life, backgrounds and locations have been in this very spot that I was residing. When you reflect on the age and the location of the Strater here in Durango Colorado, you come to appreciate that these little diaries are actually time capsules. Many famous and notable people make their stay at the Strater when they visit the Durango area.

Some of these notable people include:

- Otto Mears
- Gustaf Nordenskiold
- Will Rogers
- Louis L' Amour
- President John F. Kennedy
- Robert Kennedy
- Audie Murphy
- President Gerald Ford
- Imogene Coca
- Butch Cassidy Gang
- The Apollo 16 Astronauts
- Thomas Sefton

- Astronaut Buzz Aldrin
- Director Renny Harlin
- Francis Ford Coppola
- Linda Gray
- Lillian Russell
- Steven Spielberg
- Jerry Seinfeld
- Ralph Lauren
- Ian Tyson
- Ambassador Firestone
- Robert Redford
- Dave Brubeck

- William Conrad
- Dan Fogelberg
- Edith Mason
- Christi Brinkley
- Michael Keaton
- Chevy Chase
- Lowell Thomas
- Barry Manilow
- Film Crew from Cliffhanger
- Ralph Nader
- Tat-6 Conference
- The Grateful Dead

Every person on this list has made a lasting imprint on the history of our world as we know it today. The list varies from Presidents to Movie Stars to Astronauts.

A number of these individuals and their connection to the Strater had an actual impact on their lives and ours. I have selected a number of these individuals and their stories for this chapter.

# Who Slept in My Bed?

## Gustaf Nordenskiold 1868 – 1895

Gustaf's Nordenskiold's father Nils Adolf Erik Nordenskiold of Sweden is credited with the discovery of the long-sought after Northeast Passage in 1878-79. This is the water route along the northern coast of Europe and Asia that extended North into the Arctic Circle. Although sought after for literally centuries, he was the first man to accomplish the voyage. He did so in a ship named the Vega, a 300 ton vessel fitted with steam engines and sails, navigating for the first time the northern coasts of Europe and Asia.

*Gustaf Nordenskiold*

Gustaf was just ten years of age when his father made the discovery of the Northeast Passage. Without a doubt, this must have made a lasting impression upon Gustaf. He graduated from the Uppsala University in Stockholm (*renowned for its excellence in science*) in 1889 with a degree in mineralogy and chemistry. Gustaf also invoked the use of extensive photography with his research. Like his father and his grandfather before him, Gustaf was making quite a name for himself. He was also involved in a number of expeditions and was a published contributor to a number of Sweden's scholarly journals in mineralogy and geology.

The next year (1890) he traveled to Svalbard together with J. A. Björling and A. Klinckowström, bringing a collection of plant fossils back to the Swedish Museum of Natural History. After his return, he was diagnosed with tuberculosis and went to Berlin for treatment.[58] This was the same disease that killed his sister Maja. You can just imagine the grief his parents must have felt, when they learned of this. His father paved the way for Gustaf to travel to Berlin for medical treatment and then for Gustaf to go on a world tour. Practiced for over a century, it was believed that if a person with TB would travel to a different climate, they might be cured. With the assistance of his father, Gustaf pulled out "all stops" to apply this treatment. After traveling throughout Europe, he set sail for America. Arriving in New York, his tour of the states included Niagara Falls, Washington D.C., Chicago, Mammoth Cave, Kentucky and Denver, as well as numerous others.

While in Denver, Gustaf learned of the recently discovered ancient cliff dwellings known today as Mesa Verde. He was anxious to see these for himself, and made Durango his next destination. Gustaf arrived in Durango on Wednesday afternoon, July 1, 1891, where he stayed at the Strater House.

Upon his arrival at the 800 year old cliff dwellings, he was amazed at the archeological opportunity at the dwellings and overwhelmed at the amount of artifacts still in tact. He spent a great amount of time at the dwellings, documenting his findings and also accruing more than 600 historical treasures and artifacts. He prepared a total of 15 crates and two barrels filled with antiquities for shipment back to Sweden.

In the mean time, back in Durango, two differing factions had formed. On the one side were

# Who Slept in My Bed?

those that supported Gustaf and looked upon his work with favor. The other faction did not. The latter learned of his intentions to remove artifacts back to Sweden and were outraged! Near midnight on September 17th, 1891, they assembled a group of men with guns, and led by the town sheriff, closed in on the Strater House to arrest Gustaf for "stealing" artifacts and for "devastation of ruins at Mancos." Because there was no such law in existence at the time, they attempted to apply an old law stating that "no foreigner may travel into Indian country without a passport" - section 2134.

This arrest quickly became an international incident! Gustaf sat in Room 323 at the Strater House under house arrest. Although telephones had already been invented, they were still in their infancy. Thank goodness for telegraph. Transatlantic cables had already been laid decades earlier, so Gustaf could wire home for assistance. His Message: *"Much Troble.....No Danger..... Send Money...."* His family was a very influential family. A total of 14 American and Swedish officials became involved with this controversy including the U.S. Attorney General and the Secretary of State.

**Arrest of a Baron.**

Durango.Sept.18.—Baron Mordenskidd. of Stockholm, Sweden, was arrested at the Strater hotel, last night by Deputy United States Marshal Sargent, charged with robbing the cliff dwellings, of the Ute Indian reservation of relics, etc. The information was furnished by Agent Bartholomew, who came up from Ignacio for this purpose. The Indians have often reported and warned the Swedish baron. The baron came here direct from Sweden about six weeks ago, and obtained permission to go on the reservation to explore the ruins of the cliff dwellers, but with the understanding that he was not to molest or remove anything. Contrary to this, it seems that the baron fitted out a party of eight men and went at once to digging and tearing down these ancient ruins, carrying an immense amount of relics, pottery, skeletons and implements, boxing and shipping them by express to New York, where they were to be shipped, and that the work has been one of general devastation to those interesting land marks of a race long dead. The baron is held awaiting the action of the proper authorities.

*News Article from the Aspen News*
*Sep 19, 1891*

**Photo taken by Gustaf Nordenskiold in 1891. It is here that Gustaf carried out excavations in Soda Canyon. Rooms such as this were built in the most inaccessible locations.**

*Courtesy of Gustaf Nordenskiold Mesa Verde 1891*
*Museovirasto National Board of Antiquities * Helsinki*

# Who Slept in My Bed?

Communication between the various officials from both countries was proactive in Gustaf's behalf. By the time the case came to trial on Monday October 5th, the charges were dropped, almost before the trial even started. The leading plaintiff and his attorney didn't even show up and were no where to be found!

Gustaf stayed on in Durango and Mesa Verde for two more weeks taking extensive photographs of the cliff dwellings with a newly acquired camera that he had ordered. He had his collection of 600 artifacts loaded onto Denver & Rio Grande railroad boxcars in Durango and shipped to Europe. His collection is on display to this day at the National Museum in Helsinki, Finland.

In the end, Nordenskiöld took more than 150 photographs of Mesa Verde, logged multiple sites, and in 1893, published one of the first books about Mesa Verde, *The Cliff Dwellers of Mesa Verde, Southwestern Colorado: Their Pottery and Implements*, a monumental report of his excavations, describing in detail the buildings, pottery, skeletal remains, and tools found at the sites. Former Mesa Verde National Park superintendent Robert Heyder summed up Gustaf Nordenskiold's contributions, stating: *"I shudder to think what Mesa Verde would be today had there been no Gustaf Nordenskiöld. It is through his book that the cliff dwellings of Mesa Verde became known and his volume might well be called the harbinger of Mesa Verde National Park as we know it today."*

*Artifacts found by Gustaf Nordenskiold in 1891. (1.) Stone Axe. (2.) Woven Cotton Blanket found in Mug House by Gustaf in 1891. (3.) A lidded Kiva–jar intended for hanging in the Kiva for ceremonial purposes. (4.) Black on white bowl found in Step House by Gustaf in 1891. (5.) Black on White Mug found in Mesa Verde dated between 1100—1300 A.D..*

# Who Slept in My Bed?

*Above: Cliff Palace photographed by Gustaf Nordenskiold in 1891.[49] Cliff Palace is the largest cliff dwelling of its type on the North American continent. This dwelling had a total of 217 sleeping and storage rooms and 23 ceremonial rooms. The population was over 200 residents.*

*Below: Cliff Palace as it looks today after the restoration efforts of the Civilian Conservation Corps. (CCC) that took place in 1932 . (Photo taken in 2006)*

# Who Slept in My Bed?

## <u>Will Rogers 1879—1935</u>

Will Rogers was first an Indian, a cowboy and then a national figure. He is now a legend. Born in 1879 on a large ranch in the Cherokee Nation near what later would become Oologah, Oklahoma, Will Rogers was taught by a freed slave how to use a lasso as a tool to work Texas Longhorn cattle on the family ranch.

As he grew older, Will's roping skills were so developed that he was listed in the Guinness Book of Records for throwing three lassos at once: One rope caught the running horse's neck; the other would hoop around the rider and the third swooped up under the horse to loop all four legs. Will Rogers' unsurpassed lariat feats were recorded in the classic movie, "The Ropin' Fool."

He was the star of Broadway and 71 movies of the 1920s and 1930s. He was a popular broadcaster; wrote more than 4,000 syndicated newspaper columns, and befriended Presidents, Senators and Kings.

During his lifetime, he traveled around the globe three times, meeting people, covering wars, talking about peace and learning everything possible. He wrote six books. In fact, he published more than two million words. He was the first big time radio com-

*Courtesy of Will Rogers Memorial Museum, Claremore, Okla.*

mentator, and was a guest at the White House; his opinions were sought by the leaders of the world.[50]

While a fast horse thrilled Will, he also loved flying. It was on a flight to Alaska in August, 1935 with a daring one eyed Oklahoma pilot named Wiley Post, that their plane crashed and both men lost their lives. Just three weeks before that fateful crash, Will had spent some time in Durango at the Strater. This rare photo of Wiley's plane was taken during that final stay in Durango in 1935. At the time of his visit, Earl Sr. was Durango's Mayor and Earl Jr., who was just a six year old boy at the time, was afforded the opportunity to sit on Will's knee and hear a story.

During his stay at the Strater, Will found out that the Hotel staff were replacing the elevator car with an upgrade, so with the encouragement of the management, he carved his name in the elevator wall. He stated that he had always had a hankering to do so, and was happy to oblige. The section with his name was cut out and saved.

*Courtesy of Roderick E. Barker*

189

# Who Slept in My Bed?

## Louis L'Amour 1908—1988

Louis L'Amour, like many others living during this era, had a limited education. Although he had left school in the 10th grade, Louis had a thirst for knowledge. Throughout his life, Louis hunted libraries and bookstores across the country and all over the world. Often he went without meals in order to afford to buy books. He sometimes worked long and hard so that he could quit working temporarily and afford to study full time. Louis was proud of the fact that from 1928 until 1942, he read more than 150 non-fiction books a year and that in order to do it, he worked miserable jobs and lived in skid row hotels and campgrounds.

*Louis L'Amour at the typewriter in his Los Angeles apartment in 1953*

Louis, in time became a very famous writer. From short stories to poems to novels. Examples of his works include: "Down The Long Hills", for which he won the Western Writers of America's Golden Spur Award, and also, the North Dakota's Theodore Roosevelt Rough Rider Award. His novels "Hondo" and "Flint" are voted places in the 25 best Western Novels of all time. Five years after out selling John Steinbeck's total of 41,300,000 copies (a Bantam record) Louis L'Amour sold his one hundred millionth book and had won the Western Writer's of America's Golden Saddleman Award. In 1983 U.S. Congress voted him the National Gold Medal, and a year later the Medal of Freedom. Louis' books have been translated into over fifteen foreign languages and are sold in English in almost a dozen countries. By the year 2000, 12 years after his death, over sixty million copies of his books had been sold. Most of his collections of short stories have become hardcover best sellers.[51]

Starting in 1966, Louis L'Amour would take his family to spend the summer in Durango, Colorado, a place he had visited briefly with a mining buddy back in the late 1920s. For over 10 years they spent the month of August at the Strater Hotel. The room of choice for Louis and his wife Kathy was always room 222, and his children Beau and Angelique stayed in room 223. Louis divided his time between writing in this corner room over the Diamond Belle Saloon and hiking in the La Plata or San Juan Mountains.

Louis was a fan of all things western and had a great appetite for immersing himself in the culture. Durango and the Strater fit the bill perfectly. Louis was never far off from a good reference library and traveled with a trunk full of books and writing materials. This is well remembered by Rod Barker who was a bellman during many of his stays in the early 70's. The trunk took two bellmen to lift and carry it up the flight of stairs to the room. The L'Amour family visit became a highlight for the entire hotel staff as they became like family.

*This is room 222, Louis L'Amour's favorite room at the Strater. He sat at this table writing many of his books including the famous Western series entitled "The Sacketts".*

# Who Slept in My Bed?

Welcome to Room 222. As you may know, Louis and I spent many nights in this room here at the Strater.

Because of our love of Durango, and especially this hotel, we came back year after year, always choosing our favorite room: 222.

Louis wrote many books during our stays at this hotel. Because you are now a guest in Room 222, you are receiving one of the books whose story line was set in this area.

I hope you have a wonderful visit and enjoy yourselves here as much as we always did.

Sincerely,

Kathy L'Amour

## Audie Murphy 1924—1971

Audie Murphy served as an American Soldier during World Was II. He was in active duty for a total of 27 months. Within that short period of time, he became the most decorated combat soldier of World War II. When he enlisted, he stood only 5' 5" tall and weighed in at only 112 pounds. His small stature was no comparison to his bravery and courage.  Please note the *Citation* below:

*Citation—Second Lt. Murphy commanded Company B, which was attacked by six tanks and waves of infantry. Lt. Murphy ordered his men to withdraw to prepared positions in a woods, while he remained forward at his command post and continued to give fire directions to the artillery by telephone. Behind him, to his right, one of our tank destroyers received a direct hit and began to burn. Its crew withdrew to the woods. Lt. Murphy continued to direct artillery fire, which killed large numbers of the advancing enemy infantry. With the enemy tanks abreast of his position, Lt. Murphy climbed on the burning tank destroyer, which was in danger of blowing up at any moment, and employed its .50 caliber machine gun against the enemy. He was alone and exposed to German fire from three sides, but his deadly fire killed dozens of Germans and caused their infantry attack to waver. The enemy tanks, losing infantry support, began to fall back. For an hour the Germans tried every available weapon to eliminate Lt. Murphy, but he continued to hold his position and wiped out a squad that was trying to creep up unnoticed on his right flank. Germans reached as close as 10 yards, only to be mowed down by his fire. He received a leg wound, but ignored it and continued his single-handed fight until his ammunition was exhausted. He then made his way back to his company, refused medical attention, and organized the company in a counterattack, which forced the Germans to withdraw. His directing of artillery fire wiped out many of the enemy; he killed or wounded about 50. Lt. Murphy's indomitable courage and his refusal to give an inch of ground saved his company from possible encirclement and destruction, and enabled it to hold the woods which had been the enemy's objective.*

*1955 photo of Audie Murphy and his wife, Pam Archer Murphy, as they arrived at the Los Angeles premiere of "To Hell and Back" at the Wiltern Theater on October 12, 1955.*[53]

After the war, Audie Murphy starred in a number of movies. His highest grossing film was "*To Hell and Back*," an autobiographical film in which he starred as himself. The film grossed almost ten million dollars during its initial theatrical release, and at the time became Universal's biggest hit of the studio's entire 43-year history. This movie held the record as the company's highest-grossing motion picture until 1975, when it was finally surpassed by Steven Spielberg's "*Jaws*".[52]

Murphy enjoyed an extended stay at the Strater and later at the home of Earl and Jentra Barker while filming the 1957 movie *"Night Passage"*.


## Thomas W. Sefton 1917—2006

A very well known and respected man that loved the Strater Hotel was Tom Sefton, owner of the San Diego Savings and Trust Banks, a nearly 2 billion dollar business. He would frequent the Strater along with his son Harley, staying at the Strater for months at a time from the late 1960's until his death in 2006. Their special room was 400. He loved Colorado and also had a cabin up in the La Plata Mountains, west of town.

Tom's love for the outdoors and nature was instilled in his son Harley as well. As a young boy, Harley loved to catch chipmunks that frequented the woods around the cabin. On one particular day, Harley had a rather impressive catch of 7 or 8 of the little fellows and decided to show them to his friends in town. They were in a little wire covered box with a trap door. While away from the room, a young Puerto Rican housekeeper accidently bumped open the door and they all escaped from the box and proceeded to run around the room and down the 4th floor hallway. This got the attention of the entire Strater staff that were also running here and there with boxes and bags attempting to herd and catch all the critters back into captivity. It was quite a scene, with several women safely standing on chairs to avoid the possibility of being touched by the chipmunks.

# Who Slept in My Bed?

Tom Sefton was an interesting and unique person. He was born Oct. 8, 1917 in New York to a Scotch/Irish family. At the young age of just two months old, he became a orphan. He was adopted as an infant by Joseph W. Sefton Jr. and his wife, Helen. His adopted father must have been a no nonsense type of person. I found it very interesting that he put in a shooting range on the top floor of the bank. It's purpose: "So that everyone would know how to shoot straight in case of a robbery." The picture to the right is a photo of the females who were employed by the bank practicing their aim.

*The Bank's shooting range on the top floor.*

Although the San Diego Trust & Savings Bank was a business started by his (adopted) grandfather, Tom's first job in the bank was a messenger. This was in 1938. He was 20 years old. Tom was paid literally half of what other messengers were being paid, just $40.00 per month! After 13 years of hard work, in 1951 he eventually was promoted to the position of Vice President. Seven years later in 1958, he was promoted to Senior Vice President. Thereafter, he was eventually put in charge of the bank empire. With Tom Sefton at the helm, the San Diego Trust grew to include 53 branches with assets of $1.4 billion. At the time of his retirement after the bank's 100th anniversary, it was the primary financial institution of 10 percent of San Diego County households.

Rod Barker has fond memories of Tom. He told me that Tom was a warm and caring fellow who was viewed as member of the Strater family. He would stay for weeks at a time either up at the cabin or here at the Strater in Room 400. Tom would come down for breakfast each morning and take the time and effort necessary to learn the name of nearly every hotel staff member. He had a penchant for names and soon knew more local Durangoans by name than most natives. As a banker, Tom made it his business to know people and take a personnel interest in them. Because of this, he became one of the most loved visitors in Durango. He not only knew names, but the names of spouses and children and even the businesses that they worked for.

*Thomas W. Sefton*

His love for trains might have factored into his love for Durango. Durango is famous for it's historic narrow gauge railroad that continues to run between Silverton and Durango to this day.

Tom Sefton had a model train collection that literally staggers the imagination. It consisted of some 7,000 toy trains and accessories. Today, the collection can be viewed at the California State Railroad Museum.

Life is all about relationships. Rod Barker fully appreciates this truth. Befriending Tom and his son Harley, Rod continues to be close friends with Harley. Whenever he visits Durango, he stays at the Strater and makes it a point to try and experience the charm and appeal of a different room on each stay.

# Who Slept in My Bed?

## President John F. Kennedy 1917—1963

The 35th president of the United States, John F. Kennedy holds a place in the hearts of millions to this day. I distinctly remember the events of November 22, 1963 when he was murdered by an assassin's bullets in Dallas Texas.

**JFK campaigning on the front steps of the Strater.**

Although the way he died is indelibly inscribed in our mind's eye, the legacy of his life and the activities of his short term in office still affect our lives to this day. A number of these are listed below:

1. JFK's moral leadership of Civil Rights was an important part of the movement's eventual success. Kennedy used executive orders and personal appeals to aid the movement.
2. The Cuban Missile Crisis, which could have led to a Nuclear conflict with Russia was aborted by President Kennedy.
3. The Peace Corp was established by John F. Kennedy under Executive Order No. 10924 on March 1, 1961. More than 195,000 people have served as Peace Corp volunteers in 139 countries. President Carter's wife served as a nurse in the program and considered it "one of the most glorious experiences of her life."[54]
4. Kennedy also agreed to a Nuclear Test Ban Treaty in 1963 with Britain and the USSR.
5. There are many other notable events that are well documented regarding President Kennedy.

Turning our attention to 1960, John F. Kennedy was on the campaign trail for the Presidency of the United States. He came to Durango Colorado while on the campaign trail during the month of June, in 1960. Although there were many hotels to choose from, his choice was the Strater Hotel. His stayed in Room 322. He also made extensive use of the facilities during his stay, even setting up "shop" for his staff downstairs and delivering a speech in the Gold Room. *(The Gold Room was remodeled in 1987 and renamed the Pullman Room.)*

Durango was hosting the State Democratic Convention on Saturday, June 18, 1960. The Convention was held in the gym at nearby Fort Lewis College.

Part of J.F.K.'s speech here in Durango included these words: "It was Theodore Roosevelt who said that "To waste, to destroy, our natural resources.... will result in undermining in the days of our children the very prosperity which we ought by right to hand down to them amplified and developed." That distinguished Republican President possessed a vision and an understanding which his successors have lost. For today's Republicans have neglected and undermined the natural heritage, the hope for prosperity, of our children. Only under a new Democratic Administration - an Administration which will apply creative and dynamic principles of planning and financing to old problems and historic programs - can we begin to amplify and develop the abundance we have been so freely given. Only under a Democratic Administration will we realize the prophecy of Stephen Douglas who, a hundred years ago, said of the "Great West" and its wealth - "There, is the hope of this nation."

# Who Slept in My Bed?

*These photos were taken while John F. Kennedy and his entourage were downstairs in the Gold Room (which became the Pullman Room) at the Strater Hotel in 1960.*

*Courtesy of Roderick E. Barker*

# Who Slept in My Bed?

The TAT-6 Conference under way in the Gold Room (Now named the Pullman Room) at the Strater Hotel. This international meeting helped to change the way the world communicates. The Conference Program of Events was dated October 29th through November 4th, 1972.

## The TAT-6 Conference

Global communications as we know it today has only been possible for a relatively short period of time. The first transatlantic telegraph cables were originally laid in 1858. They only functioned for one month before communications stopped. It wasn't until 1866, nine years later that a successful connection was obtained. This system however, was limited to Morse code.

Then in 1927, a radio-based transatlantic telephone system was established. The cost was extremely high. A three minute call cost $45! The average industrial wage per week in America at that time was $23—$25. So it would have cost just about two weeks worth of wages to pay for a three minute phone call to Europe!

As time progressed, technology continued to advance. By the middle of the twentieth century, discoveries and understanding made it not only possible, but also affordable to put into place a modern communications program that could eventually connect the entire globe.

On December 1, 1953, the announcement was made by the Postmaster General that an agreement had been made to lay the first Transatlantic cable establishing standard telephone communications between Europe and America. This would be a joint project between the General Post Office of the UK, the American Telephone and Telegraph Company (AT&T) and the Canadian Overseas Telecommunications Corporation.

Over the summers of 1955 and 1956, the first submarine telecommunications cables capable of connecting individuals voice to voice between Europe and America were laid. The first public telephone calls were completed on September 25, 1956. TAT-1 carried 588 London-US calls

# Who Slept in My Bed?

and 119 London-Canada calls in the first 24 hours of public service. The maximum load was 36 simultaneous calls at any one time.

Despite this advancement, international communication was still only in its infancy. An example that underscores this is the Cuban Missile Crisis of 1963. Direct communications between the two superpowers, the U.S.A. and Russia, had not yet been established. During the crisis, it took the U.S. nearly 12 hours to receive and decode Russian leader Nikita Khrushchev's 3,000 word initial settlement message. This was a dangerously long time to have Nikita Khrushchev wait in silence, without a reply, while at the brink of Nuclear War! By the time the U.S. had decoded the message and drafted a reply, a tougher message from Moscow was received demanding that U.S. missiles be removed from Turkey. This, all because of the fact that man had already developed and implemented ways to destroy the planet, but not how to communicate with each other! What a sad testament to our priorities.

Thankfully, after TAT-1 was accomplished, ongoing improvements and newer technologies continued to be implemented. TAT's-2,3,4 & 5 all added greatly to the communications capability potentials that mankind was beginning to enjoy.

In the fall of 1972, attempts were made to move forward with Tat-6. Because of political issues and the public press interference, initial attempts had failed. One fellow raised the suggestion of holding the conference in a small hotel that he was familiar with, located out West in a small town named Durango. He felt that in this location, they would be able to avoid the publicity and the political pressures and perhaps come to a final resolve regarding the Tat-6 Conference agendas.

The suggestion was a big hit! Earl Barker Jr. got all the preliminaries and the extracurricular activities set up for the Conference members, including a Rodeo, a Western Bar-B-Q and music. This took some doing, because cowboys don't usually do rodeos at that time of the year. They don't like to Rodeo in the snow and the cold!

Starting on October 29th thru November 4th 1972, the international parties involved convened at the Strater Hotel in Durango Colorado for the TAT-6 Conference. It was determined here at the Strater, that the cable would be laid between the U.S.A. and France. Their intentions would make all the accomplishments up to that time pale in significance! After production, development and installation, TAT-6 went into service in 1976 and was in service through 1994. Running from Rhode Island to France, this telecommunications cable, - TAT-6, could handle nearly four times the load of calls of the entire first 5 TAT Cables combined! TAT-6 had a final number of 10,000 channels while the entire previous 5 had a total sum of 2,853.

Today, new technologies have replaced the Galvanic cables originally installed through TAT's 1—7 with Fiber Optics. Starting with TAT-8 in 1988, fiber optics began to be incorporated. Though thinner than human hair, optical fiber carries so much information that four fibers in a transatlantic telephone cable can handle up to 40,000 calls at once! Technology continues to develop and change the way that we communicate.

The Strater Hotel played an important role in the development of the earth-wide communications that we enjoy today.

# Who Slept in My Bed?

## The Apollo 16 Astronauts

Apollo 16 was the fifth mission to land men on the Moon and return them to Earth. It was also the second flight of the Lunar Roving Vehicle. Apollo 16 landed in a highlands area, a region not yet explored on the Moon. Astronauts collected samples, took photographs and conducted experiments that included the first use of an ultraviolet camera/spectrograph on the Moon. This flight was also a testament to the training and experience of the astronauts. From the very beginning, just after lift off from the earth's surface on April 16th, 1972, multiple issues developed that had to be considered and acted upon by the three Astronauts. Rather than canceling the mission, they continued onward completing the 11 day mission successfully.

*Taken at the Strater Hotel in the Columbian Room, this photo includes members of the Apollo 16 Crew including Young, Duke and Mattingly plus the complete Apollo 16 backup crew of Haise, Progue and Carr. Haise, Progue and Carr were destined to become the crew of Apollo 19, but this flight was cancelled in September 1970. At that time Pogue and Carr were removed from the Apollo 16 backup crew and assigned to Skylab. This unique photo was taken in the early summer of 1969.*

**All color photos on this page courtesy of N.A.S.A.**

# Chapter Ten
## 10


# Reflections

# Reflections

*There are many people* that have journeyed to the Strater and continue to do so. Rod Barker estimates that 1.5 million people have stayed at the Strater over the past 120 years. There are many reasons why individuals continue to be drawn to this unique location in Durango, Colorado. I personally appreciate the antiquity of the building, it's furnishings and atmosphere. It brings to me a peace and tranquility that is difficult to attain back home in the suburbs of Chicago, one of the largest of metropolitan areas in the United States.

Individuals go to destinations such as Universal Studios in Florida and go on virtual rides that momentarily are capable of overriding all your senses, fooling your mind to the point where it is difficult to separate reality from illusion. People go on these rides to experience this illusion.

Staying at the Strater is similar in a number of ways. When you enter the Strater, your senses are filled with the furnishings and décor of the good life more than 100 years in the past. Because of the location and small population, as compared to the "Big Cities," people "Stop and Smell the Roses" here. The pace of life is distinctly calmer and more peaceful. The chug...chug...chug of the coal powered steam locomotives add to the overwhelming feeling that you have stepped back in time. Unlike the illusion of a ride to fool the senses, this literally becomes your reality for as long as you stay at the Strater. Of course, the modern conveniences are all in place, and your level of comfort is superb. The quality of food at the Mahogany Grille will more than please the most astute palate. But that's not all; comfort and surroundings are important, but there is more. The key ingredient that brings all of these factors together into the memorable experience that it has become is the warm, friendly, extremely hospitable service and attention, that you receive from the outgoing and perceptive employees at the Strater.

Add all these factors together and you have a destination spot that you will pine for, and revisit many times over. This is why the famous writer Louis L'Amore, along with his wife Kathy and children Beau and Angelique, came for eight or nine years in a row and would stay for three months at a time.

Denny W. Viles, (*Vice President of the American Vanadium Corporation*) traveled all over the world, including Europe, Peru and Africa. He had a home in Durango on Third Avenue, but he had no family. In his later years, although he could have made any destination his home, he chose the Strater. He made room 116 his residence. The Strater "adopted" him as part of the family. Every morning, a member or two of the Strater staff would help him down the stairs for breakfast. They were always there to offer him any assistance he needed. Rod Barker told me that "*he was a tall man with glasses and not much hair, but he had a smile that you would just fall in love with.*"

These are just a few of the many stories that could be told. There are literally hundreds of others. They are recorded in the diaries found in each room, as well as in the hearts of those that work at the Strater. I encourage you to visit Durango and make the Strater your home while there. Be certain to pen your experiences in the room diary for others to appreciate. Perhaps 20, 30 or even 100 years from now, your experience will have an impact on another person looking to appreciate the serenity of the by-gone days, just as you and I do today.

# Strater Hotel Timeline

**1859**   Henry H. Strater was born in Cleveland Ohio

**1880**   Henry along with his two older brothers, Frank and Fred moved to Durango, Colo.

**1881**   The Strater Brothers built a one story building on Main Avenue and opened the Strater Brothers Paint and Oils Store.

**1882**   The Strater Brothers added a second story and extended the rear of the store making the structure four times its original size.

**1887**   Henry Strater began construction of the four story Strater Hotel. This would be the largest building in Durango for many years to come.

**1888**   The Strater Hotel opened on August 31, 1888. It became well known throughout the West as one of the most luxurious upper class hotels in the entire region.

**1889**   Durango is hit by fire that reduced eight blocks to cinders. The Strater was spared but Henry Strater and H. L. Rice both lost their homes in this blaze.

**1892**   Henry Strater was the President of the Durango Board of Trade. He was also president of the Strater-Thorpe Drug Company, with his main facility in Durango and branches in Silverton and Rico.

**1893**   Henry Strater built the Columbian hotel next door to the Strater, literally enveloping and enlarging upon the original two story Strater Paint and Oils Store. This same year, the Silver Panic hit. The Strater-Thorpe Drug Company collapsed financially.

**1894**   Henry Strater lost both hotels due to the financial crisis. The properties were foreclosed by the Bank of Cleveland and Cleveland banker John Macbeth assumed control and ownership.

**1898**   Henry Strater and his wife Carrie moved to Philadelphia.

**1900**   On May 24th, 1900, a fire started in the Strater on the fourth floor that charred much of that level and threatened the entire structure. Due to the diligence of the fire department and volunteers, the Strater was saved.

**1902**   The Strater and the Columbian hotels were joined together as one by Stilwell and Company. This was the management company of the hotels.

**1914**   Henry Strater died in Cuba at 55 years of age.

**1924**   The MacBeth family sold the Strater.

**1926**   Earl Barker Sr. purchased the Strater Hotel with a group of local business men.

**1953**   Earl Barker Sr., at the time president of Burns Bank in Durango, purchased the entire stock of the hotel. This is the first time that the owner of the hotel managed the hotel.

**1954**   Earl Barker, Jr. and Robert Blomstrom join Earl Sr. to run the Strater Hotel.

**1957**   The Barker family began the major undertaking of revitalizing the Strater. They started with the creation of the now famous Diamond Belle Saloon to begin the vision of entertainment and guest service they had for the hotel.

**1962**   The Diamond Circle Theatre, located next door to the hotel, began its first season of Melodrama with the show "The Tavern".

**1963**   Jentra Barker found a beautiful Victorian bed while accompanying her husband Earl at a convention in Atlanta. This began the process of purchasing and shipping American Victorian antiques to redecorate each room in the hotel.

**1968**   Earl Barker Jr. took over ownership of the Strater and continued with renovations giving special attention to bathrooms, air conditioning, electrical rewiring, heating and closets.

**1983**   Rod Barker returned to Durango to continue the family tradition as the third generation Manager and Designer. During the next 27+ years, Rod and Charlie Schumacher accomplished renovations of the Pullman Banquet room, the Lobby, Office Spiritorium, Centennial Room, Mahogany Grille, the Oak Room and each of the 93 rooms. Much attention was paid to guest service, comfort and great food and beverage outlets.

**2010**   Although 123 years old at the time of this writing, the Strater is in picture perfect condition. Attention to detail is the trademark that goes into everything that the Barker family operates. The Strater was the Jewel of the Rockies the day it opened in 1888, and she continues her regal reign to this day.

# Sources
# and Notes

# Sources and Notes

[1] www.legendsofamerica.com/MO-StLouis

[2] http://en.wikipedia.org/wiki/William_Greeneberry_Russell

[3] www.experiencefestival.com/a/Colorado_Gold_Rush_-_William_Green_Russell/id/1243665

[4] The Pike's Peak Gold Rush (later known as the Colorado Gold Rush) was the boom in gold prospecting and mining in the Pike's Peak Country of northwestern Kansas Territory and southwestern Nebraska Territory of the United States that began in July 1858 and lasted until roughly the creation of the Colorado Territory on February 28, 1861. An estimated 100,000 gold seekers took part in the greatest gold rush in North American history. The participants in the gold rush were known as Fifty-Niner's after 1859, the peak year of the rush. *From Wikipedia*

[5] www.uteindian.com

[6] The Man On The Iron Horse by Rhoda Davis Wilcox

[7] Ibid

[8] Ibid

[9] Ibid

[10] Pioneers of the San Juan Country by Sarah Platt Decker Chapter

[11] www.ghostdepot.com/rg/history/otto%20mears.htm

[12] Pioneers of the San Juan Country by Sarah Platt Decker Chapter

[13] Ibid

[14] Ibid

[15] Ibid

[16] Ibid

[17] Pioneers of the San Juan Country by Sarah Platt Decker Chapter

[18] Ibid

[19] Ibid

[20] Ibid

[21] Ibid

[22] Ibid

[23] Ibid

[24] Ibid

[25] Ibid

[26] Ibid

[27] Ibid

[28] Ibid

[29] Ibid

[30] Ibid

[31] Ibid

[32] Ibid

[33] Ibid

[34] Ibid

[35] Ibid

[36] Ibid

[37] Ibid

# Sources and Notes

[38]"A Hotel For All Seasons" By Duane Smith

[39] Ibid

[40] Ibid

[41] Ibid

[42] "At The Strater -100 Years of Hospitality" by Kristi Nelson with excerpts of Duane Smith's "Pride of Durango"

[43] In 1887 a farm laborer was earning $1.38 per day; a painter $2.93 per day; a bricklayer $2.94; a carpenter $2.24 and a plumber $3.52 per day. Annual non-farm employees in the U.S. made $509.—
*"Historical Statistics of the U.S. – Colonial Times to 1970"*

[44] J. Laurence Laughlin, *The History of Bimetallism in the United States*, 4th ed.

[45] Ibid

[46]MyKathy Weiser / Legends of America

[47] Better Homes and Gardens Wood Magazine  April 1998 "The Woodworker and the Hotel"

[48]My grandfather kind of panicked after Prohibition," Barker said. "He bought a railroad car full of Early Times whiskey in 1933 or '34 after prohibition ended so his guests would never again go without. That batch probably lasted 10 years or more, and we've sold it ever since. From The Durango Herald Online, By Ted Holteen\Herald Staff Writer

Research on Gustaf Nordenskiold:    1. Nordenskiold of Mesa Verde By Judith & David Reynolds
                                    2. Wikipedia

[49] Photo courtesy of Gustaf Nordenskiold Mesa Verde 1891 Museovirasto National Board of Antiquities * Helsinki

[50] www.willrogers.org, Written by Joseph H. Carter

[51]The official Louis L Amour Website at www.louislamour.com.

[52] www.hollywoodusa.co.uk

[53] www.audiemurphy.com/gallery/gallery20.htm

[54]Peace Corps On Line

[55]Identifying Eastlake Furniture by Pamela Wiggins -About.com

[56]Durango Herald, October 30, 2009—Legends Set First Tracks at Purgatory by Dale Strode

[57]www.answers.com/topic/1836 (see restaurants)

[58] Academic Dictionaries and Encyclopedias—http://en.academic.ru/dic.nsf/enwiki/1347331

# About the Author

Phil Aleo and his family live in Illinois in the northwest suburbs of Chicago. Although he resides in the Midwest, his heart is out West. He has been traveling to Colorado and the West for over 15 years, almost on an annual basis.

Having a passion for history and photography, Phil published his first book in 2002 entitled; **"Dundee Township - *Moments Frozen In Time"*.** This was a local, historical and photographic book that showcased his hometown area from its earliest days starting in the 1830's.

He states: "Without a doubt, my greatest motivation, and reward for my work, is the enthusiasm that people demonstrate. This happens quite often when they get a glimpse of a familiar place as it looked 100 years ago; or when an historical question that went unanswered perhaps for years, gets resolved. To hear their heartfelt expressions of appreciation literally brings tears to my eyes."

*Rod Barker and Phil Aleo (wearing bow tie) dressed in 1800's period clothing in 2009 during the annual Strater Open House held in April.*